To JOHN
We love you!
From Mommy + DADDY
2-4-84   HOUSTON TX
TEXAS

To JOHN
We love you!

AMERICA
and its
PRESIDENTS

AMERICA
and its
PRESIDENTS

By Earl Schenck Miers

Portraits in Color by Stanley Dersh
Line Drawings by Paul Granger

*Paintings of Gerald Ford, Jimmy Carter and Ronald Reagan
by Arnaldo Putzu in association with Artists International.*

*Additional illustrations of Gerald Ford, Jimmy Carter
and Ronald Reagan by Helen Tullen.*

Additional text material by Bea Scala.

Publishers • GROSSET & DUNLAP • New York

INTRODUCTION

Aside from John Quincy Adams, who didn't want to disappoint his parents, none of the remarkable men whose stories fill these pages planned to become President of the United States. In 1858 Abraham Lincoln laughed at the notion that any such honor ever could befall him. "In my poor, lank face," he declared, "nobody has ever seen that any cabbages were sprouting." Elected two years later to the highest office in the land, Lincoln still shook his head. What he had proved, he told a group of soldiers, was how any child in America might grow up to become President.

All types of boys — rich boys, poor boys, orphans, city kids, farm lads — became in later years the nation's Number One Citizen. If the greater number have trained for careers in law, still others have pursued a wide variety of occupations. George Washington called himself a farmer, and among those who followed him as President were two college presidents, an engineer, two professionally-trained soldiers and a pair of Indian fighters, a newspaper editor, a tailor, a shopkeeper, a city dude who loved cowpunching.

Hard work, hard thinking, hard praying — these qualities made a free country. And faith in human decency and dignity — this quality, above all others, was essential to the government of a country that existed because, as the Declaration of Independence stated, "we mutually pledge to each other our lives, our fortunes, and our sacred honor."

Wise old Thomas Jefferson had a pretty shrewd insight into the American character. "When a man assumes a public trust," Jefferson said, "he should consider himself as public property." Happily, the Presidents of the United States have agreed. Error of judgment they may have made in office, but never an error of spirit. Not all have done as well — a few have seemed exceptional, a few sad failures — but all have been men of good will, brave hearts, and devotion to our form of government as "the last, best hope of earth."

And all, without exception, have been heroes in that thrilling tale we call American history. Great decisions have rested with these men. Often, except for God, they have had to reach those decisions alone. All, probably, have recalled then the prayer that was spoken in St. Paul's Chapel in New York City after Washington's inauguration as our first President: "Almighty God, we make our earnest prayer that Thou wilt keep the United States in Thy holy protection; that Thou wilt incline the hearts of the citizens to cultivate a spirit of subordination and obedience to government; [and] to entertain a [spirit of] brotherly affection and love for their fellow-citizens of the United States at large."

From century to century this prayer echoes through our history. It is the only proper beginning to the story of America and its Presidents.

Earl Schenck Miers

ISBN 0-448-12325-8
Library of Congress Catalogue No.: 70-75327
Copyright © 1959, 1961, 1964, 1966, 1969 by Earl Schenck Miers.
Additional text copyright © 1982 by Grosset & Dunlap, Inc.
Illustrations copyright © 1959, 1961, 1964, 1966, 1969, 1982 by Grosset & Dunlap, Inc.
All rights reserved. Published simultaneously in Canada
Printed in the United States of America.

CONTENTS

COLOR PORTRAITS OF THE PRESIDENTS

GEORGE WASHINGTON

"Father of His Country"

THE ROYAL GOVERNOR of Virginia looked with approval at the young man. There was character in that face, Governor Dinwiddie decided. A lithe, hard-muscled body, steady eyes, a firm mouth, an intelligent forehead—every detail he observed convinced him that George Washington was the right man for an extremely dangerous mission.

Dinwiddie had questions to ask. Did Washington understand the great risks involved? Unless the French were stopped from stringing military posts along the Ohio River, and from inciting Indians to murder or kidnap English settlers, a war would result! Did he understand that this expedition had two objectives—to warn the French and to select proper sites for forts in case of war? How far Washington must travel to reach the French commandant was anybody's guess. The distance could be five hundred miles—or a thousand—through strange mountains and forests alive with Indians, bears and rattlesnakes!

7

If Washington wished to bow out, Dinwiddie provided the chance.
"Give me my instructions, sir," Washington said.

Dinwiddie smiled. A man for a crisis was never easy to find.

Twenty-one years had passed since George's birth in Westmoreland County, Virginia. Most of his boyhood had been spent at Ferry Farm, across from the village of Fredericksburg. He had sailed the gentle, winding Rappahannock River. On horseback he had explored the green hills nearby—or, gun in hand, had searched for fox, wolf and deer. His father's death, when George was eleven, changed that part of his life and soon a favorite half-brother, Lawrence, asked him to come live at Mount Vernon.

So George moved to that beautiful tidewater country along the Potomac known as the Northern Neck where, everyone said, even a saint couldn't get along with testy, influential Lord Fairfax. George did. The lad's strength and vigor, his ease in handling horses, his skill on a fox hunt, his quiet, shy politeness delighted the tart old nobleman. As a surveyor for Fairfax, George crossed the Blue Ridge Mountains. He knew the ways of frontiersman and Indian, one reason why Governor Dinwiddie wanted him to lead the present expedition. And after Lawrence's death, George had again shown leadership, for he had taken over the management of Mount Vernon without a hitch.

The rare combination of abilities that one day would make George Washington "the father of his country" became clear that bitter winter of 1753-54 when, at the Governor's request, he journeyed from Williamsburg, Virginia to the Indian country of western Pennsylvania. With tact and skill he carried out his mission as a wilderness diplomat. The Indians liked and trusted him. Frontiersmen nodded when he picked a point on a river where a fort should stand. He was neither fooled nor frightened by the bluster of Chabert de Joincare, sly half-breed son of a French father and Seneca mother, who was determined to drive the British from the Ohio wilderness.

The journey home was a true measure of Washington. Icy winds

howled through the mountains and snow deepened in the passes. Wait—the trip is impossible—many counseled. Washington shook his head. There was no time to spare in dealing with the land-grabbing French. He must travel to Virginia—hard and fast.

Washington returned to Williamsburg in frosty January. Along Duke of Gloucester Street ice covered the mud-holes, but the sight of the British flag spanking above the Capitol warmed Washington. His loyalty to the king in far-off England was intense, a part of his inheritance as a Virginian. It wasn't a long ride from Williamsburg to Jamestown where, in 1607, the British had planted their first permanent settlement in America. But then, riding down the peninsula between the York and James rivers, it wasn't a long ride to Yorktown where one October day Washington would turn the world upside down for the British.

Now, guessing nothing of how the future would change him completely, Washington burned only with a passion to rid the Ohio frontier of the treacherous French. And the war that Washington foresaw came within a year. Again he set out for the Ohio River, this time leading a little band of Virginia militia so poorly equipped that to call it an army was ridiculous. Other Virginians were sent ahead to build a fort on the Ohio Forks near present-day Pittsburgh.

Disaster awaited Washington. The French, no military fools, captured the half-finished bastion, then completed it for themselves. Fort Duquesne, heavily armed and guarded, provided the base from which the French ultimately defeated Washington's militiamen at Great Meadows. Unable to read French, Washington accepted unduly harsh terms of surrender. He returned to Mount Vernon, deeply stung by public criticism.

The French and Indian Wars followed. In February, 1755, General Edward Braddock arrived from Great Britain to lead the Virginia troops. By hot July Braddock's army approached Fort Duquesne, but a bull-doggishness in Braddock made it impossible for him to accept advice. Washington tried to explain frontier fighting. Behind any tree, boulder, ledge or hill—Braddock should expect to find the Indians and French there.

And that's where they were. All at once they seemed to rise from the ground, surrounding Braddock. Bright British uniforms made splendid targets for humming arrows and flashing guns. Braddock's dead littered the ground. The moans of his wounded filled the air. In terror, whole regiments bolted like wild cattle. Washington held his troops under control. Not ashamed to use the tricks of forest warfare, he avoided capture, proving himself a seasoned soldier.

For the next three years Washington continued the weary wilderness campaigns until the French and Indian Wars ended in Virginia. Gladly he returned to Mount Vernon to resume his life as a farmer and to marry Martha Dandridge Custis. The next ten years made him, in a way, a poor prospect as a patriot. His plantation prospered as he sent large shipments of tobacco to England and imported British goods. He believed it was reasonable for the British to argue that since the French and Indian Wars had involved enormous expense, the American colonists should pay taxes for their own protection.

Elected by his neighbors to represent them in Virginia's House of Burgesses, Washington came each year to Williamsburg. He loved this town with its horse races, fairs, theaters, taverns, shops and good dinners. He liked to attend the balls in the Governor's Palace and watch the bowlers on the town green. In Williamsburg he was respected as a successful planter and a stalwart member of the cautious "Old Guard."

But Williamsburg attracted all kinds. Take tough-minded Richard Henry Lee for one—he opposed slavery. Or George Wythe, America's first professor of law, who taught a Negro servant to read Latin and Greek. Or that upstart in the greased pigtail—Patrick Henry—who sniffed that a king was no better than his laws. Or young Tom Jefferson, his head overflowing with ideas—some of them bordering on outright revolution. Or a dozen others, some set in the old ways and others filled with notions about all men being created equal.

Rarely has there been a town or a time in America where a man's mind became so exposed to ideas fated to shake the world. Washington, as part of this exciting time and town, listened, argued and changed.

An astonishing thing happened. When, in 1765, the Stamp Act (with its tax on just about everything but the air colonists breathed) began a decade of crisis, leaders like Washington wanted only to cling to their rights as Englishmen. A respect for representative government, a belief in the supremacy of law, a devotion to the liberty of the individual—were these not the hard-won rights of every subject of the king?

First the Stamp Act, then interference with trial by jury, then the quartering of troops in cities, then the closing of the port of Boston—for Washington each emergency brought him back to the fundamental question. Why must any self-respecting Englishman be treated this way? When the port of Boston was closed, Virginia proclaimed a day of fasting and prayer for her sister colony. As Washington knelt in church that day, a cycle was completed. His defiance now was that of a self-respecting American, a Virginian making common cause with the man of Massachusetts! Not any one deed, but the impact of all of them led a Massachusetts man, John Adams, to say:

"The Revolution was effected before the war commenced. The Revolution was in the minds and hearts of the people."

Certainly it was fought in Washington's mind and heart during the years between the Stamp Act and the Declaration of Independence. When in May, 1775, he walked into the Philadelphia State House, where the Second Continental Congress was meeting, no one could doubt his choice. Washington came dressed in the blue and buff uniform of a colonel of the Virginia militia and wise John Adams started the move to name him Commander-in-chief of the Continental army. Washington declared that he was not "equal" to the command, but he took it.

The American Revolution was a long, bitter, heart-breaking struggle. Against Britain's well-equipped troops Washington fought with a ragtag

army of farmer-soldiers who wanted each spring to go home to their plowing. The cruel winter at Valley Forge, when ragged, hungry soldiers died in the snow, symbolized Washington's constant discouragements. People living comfortably at home refused to pay taxes for the proper support of his army. Everywhere Tories acted as spies for the British. The sheer force of Washington's dogged determination kept the Continentals fighting. And the sheer force of his keen mind won the war.

For Washington possessed one quality that above all else made him a great general. He knew when to attack, to retreat, to spring a surprise. Like a chess game, wars often are won in those moments when an opponent becomes confused over the next move.

In that exact situation Washington caught the British in 1781. American and British armies both fought that summer in New York and Virginia. To the British on Manhattan Island the logical expectation was for Washington to march his army into New Jersey and launch an attack across Staten Island. Washington gave every appearance of doing precisely that. Too late, the British realized that they had been tricked! Washington, swinging clear around New York, raced to join Lafayette in Virginia and thus to trap the British under Cornwallis inside Yorktown! That blow virtually ended the war.

Happily Washington returned to farming at Mount Vernon where his wife, despite his fame, called him her "old man." But the "free and independent states" that Washington had helped to create seethed with unrest. Congress was without leadership and almost without power. Its paper money bought next to nothing while tariffs cut off trade between states. Sadly Washington wrote to a friend: "There are combustibles in every State which a spark might set fire to."

When the Constitutional Convention was called, Washington attended as a delegate from Virginia, but his great prestige made him the natural presiding officer in a convention that, somewhat to its own surprise, soon embarked on plans for more than bolstering a weak congress. Out of long months of heated and often abusive debate a new form of government began to emerge. Washington supported a strong central government controlled by wealthy, educated men, but he scorned Alexander Hamilton's proposals for establishing a monarchy with a titled aristocracy.

Washington could not escape history. He was the miracle-worker who had won independence and men of differing opinions looked to him for leadership. The new Constitution stirred deep fears. The states were reluctant to give up power to a central authority and village people and small landowners howled that the Constitutional Convention had been used by aristocrats to steal the country. In the end, all debate settled on one compromise. All right, friend and foe said, maybe this new government would work with Washington as President.

In New York City gay crowds jammed Broad Street to witness Washington's inauguration. Bands blared. Flag-bedecked boats in the harbor boomed a salute. On the balcony of the Federal Building that bright day in 1789, Washington waited, feeling faint and ill, for the responsibility soon to rest upon his shoulders seemed too much for any man. Yet in a firm voice he took the oath of office.

Everything that occurred during Washington's two terms in office became a "first" in American history.

He appointed the first Cabinet (Thomas Jefferson, Alexander Hamilton, Henry Knox and Edmund Randolph). The first new states were admitted to the Union (Vermont, Kentucky and Tennessee).

14

The Supreme Court met for the first time, the National Mint was established, the first census was taken.

And the first ten amendments to the Constitution—the Bill of Rights—were adopted.

In 1794 a strange little war broke out in western Pennsylvania. Angry farmers, who made their corn and rye crops into whisky, denounced a Federal tax on whisky makers. When Washington sent officers to enforce the law, the Whisky Rebellion flared into open warfare between United States marshals and rebel farmers. Some were killed, some wounded. Two rebels were convicted of treason, but Washington later pardoned them. Federal authority had prevailed, but many ridiculed Washington as a high-handed aristocrat who cared nothing for the common man. These grumbles would increase. Men seeking election would repeat them. A two-party political system was beginning.

Actually through taxes, especially upon imported goods, Washington helped many American businesses develop. Convinced that he was right, he could be an immovable man. Despite popular feeling for the French Revolution, Washington distrusted it as a movement of the rabble and issued a proclamation of strict neutrality. His enemies increased. He was called a tyrant, a hypocrite, and Vice-President John Adams said he was "an old mutton head." Washington didn't conceal his pleasure when his eight years in the Presidency ended and he could retire to Mount Vernon.

In December, 1799, Washington caught a cold that developed into high fever and a sore throat. After the fashion of the day, doctors bled him. Washington knew the end was near and spoke his last words:

"I thank you for your attention; you had better not take any more trouble about me, but let me go quietly."

Washington's death shocked the nation. People wept as though a member of their family had passed away. They loved him—and would always love him.

JOHN ADAMS

"The Atlas of Independence"

A SHORT, stout man with ruddy cheeks bustled along the street, his nose set like a rudder in a straight course. Neighbors nodded respectfully and John Adams responded with a vague smile. Behind his back neighbors joked: "In a town called Braintree, someone has to be all brain."

For more than a century people in the Old Bay Colony had lived with Adamses who were tall or short, cheerful or moody. The first member of the family, Henry Adams, had reached Massachusetts in 1636, and, settling on forty acres of land in Braintree, had raised corn, beans, cows, hogs and eight sons. John Adams, born in 1735, spent his boyhood on the farm that great-grandfather Henry started ninety-nine years before.

John was raised by stern New England standards. He feared the Lord. He obeyed his parents. He thought twice before spending a shilling and then didn't spend it. He studied diligently, for as the eldest son he was expected to attend Harvard. Not yet twenty, John graduated from college, ranking fourteenth in a class of twenty-four. Harvard in those days classified graduates according to the social standing of their parents, and John prided himself on being "well-born."

The New England aristocrat, like the Virginia aristocrat, took seriously the responsibility that went with wealth and education. The New Englander generally felt less bound in allegiance to the king, but then he owed less thanks to the king for gaining a foothold in America. Still, had you asked John Adams what he thought of new-fangled notions about the equality of men, he would have answered: "Nonsense." A farmer should be content hoeing corn while the "upper classes" handled government.

Anyone who cared to quarrel with the ideas of John Adams could expect a tongue-lashing—most of all on that day in 1765 when he bustled along the streets of Braintree. Those who looked sharply saw anger pinching the corners of his mouth. And John Adams *was* mad—*fighting* mad—at the British Parliament which had passed the Stamp Act. Among the items subject to the new tax were legal documents, and as a lawyer Adams felt British fingers reaching straight into his pocketbook.

"This tax," he stormed, "was set on foot for my ruin."

And he said a great deal more. At a meeting in Braintree, ready to lick ten times his weight in British lions, he thundered that any tax to which the people had not consented was illegal. At a meeting in Boston he spoke with the same indignation. More than forty Massachusetts towns sent petitions to England protesting against the Stamp Act. John Adams's ideas were reflected in all of them.

Five years later British troops fired upon an unruly mob, killing five citizens in the famous "Boston Massacre," and neighbors learned another side of John Adams. Intense unpopularity was the best reward any lawyer could expect for defending Captain Preston and the seven British soldiers charged with these "murders." But John Adams never lacked moral courage. He studied the facts and believed the charges unjust. Nor did Adams lack common sense. He waited seven months for the public's temper to cool before going into court and absolving Preston and five soldiers of the crime. The other two, found guilty of manslaughter, were branded on the hand with a hot iron.

John Adams never received a word of gratitude from Preston for saving the captain from this torture. What did it matter? Adams acted by his own conscience, and the devil take anyone who didn't like it. In 1773, when the Boston Tea Party shocked many New Englanders with its open defiance of the king (and the waste of good tea), John Adams believed that what those tea-dumpers had done was "magnificent."

In succeeding years there wasn't a busier patriot in Revolutionary America. Who persuaded the Second Continental Congress to accept New England's sixteen thousand minutemen as the "Continental Army"? John Adams! Who worked vigorously to have Washington appointed Commander-in-chief? John Adams! When Richard Henry Lee of Virginia moved that "these United Colonies are, and of right ought to be, free and independent states," who seconded that bold resolution? John Adams! Who insisted that Thomas Jefferson was the man best qualified to write the Declaration of Independence? John Adams! Who wrote the Massachusetts Bill of Rights that became a model copied by other states? John Adams, called by Jefferson "the Atlas of American Independence"!

Beginning in 1778, John Adams served for ten years on numerous missions to Europe. Square-jawed, quick-tempered, strong-minded, he soon suspected that the French minister, Count Vergennes, had no real interest in American independence. France, guessed Adams, was playing a shrewd game by supporting our war as a means of destroying British power, after which France intended to help Spain gain control of all territory between the Allegheny Mountains and the Mississippi River. Even wise old Ben Franklin had been hoodwinked by Vergennes, decided Adams, who thought he knew how to deal with a trickster—out-trick him!

And Adams did. He negotiated a treaty with the Dutch Government that recognized American independence and France was no longer our only friend in Europe. To make this triumph sweeter, Adams also secured a Dutch loan of $2,000,000. With the aid of John Jay, he arranged a secret treaty with Britain that recognized our territorial rights in the Mississippi

Valley. He had beaten Count Vergennes at the sly art of diplomacy!

During the eight years that Washington was President, Adams held office as Vice-President. The adulation of the people for Washington annoyed him. Why, Washington hadn't contributed nearly as much as he had to the struggle for independence! Yet Adams, swallowing his personal vanity, made a fine Vice-President and stanchly supported Washington's policies.

But angry clashes developed as Americans began to divide into two political factions. Adams stood with the Federalists, who later became the Whigs and then the Republicans. Generally, the Federalists believed in a strong government run by the "well-born," which suited Adams. He opposed the French Revolution as a dangerous popular movement, coming thus to an open break with Jefferson, a supporter of the French uprising. In 1797 Washington refused to serve a third term, and Adams became the logical candidate of the Federalists. Opposing him was Jefferson, leader of the political group first known as the Republicans and afterward as the Democrats.

Jealousies, long simmering in the political pot of the Federalists, now boiled over. Alexander Hamilton, who lacked the popularity to win the nomination, looked upon Adams as an unpleasant, aggressive pighead. Hamilton schemed to divide the electoral college vote evenly between Adams and Thomas Pinckney of South Carolina so that Congress could decide which should be President. Conspiring with Southern Federalists in Congress, Hamilton hoped to make Pinckney the President, but eighteen New Englanders, seeing through the plot, voted for Adams and not for Pinckney. As a result Adams, the Federalist, became President and Jefferson, the Republican-Democrat, became Vice-President. Clearly something was wrong with a political system whereby at the death of a president the executive power passed to the opposition party!

Not that Adams intended to die before he got the better of his enemies, and as President he faced enemies everywhere. Britain and France, at war, both resented our policy of neutrality and both insisted on the right to seize American ships on the high seas. When we protested, French diplomats demanded bribes for themselves and a loan of $10,000,000 for their country to stop these acts of piracy. John Adams was a bad target for blackmail. Substituting the letters X, Y, Z for the names of the diplomats, he published their outrageous proposals.

Indignation swept America. "Millions for defense, but not one cent for tribute!" shouted the people.

Washington was called from Mount Vernon to command the army in a possible war against France.

We built a few excellent frigates, the beginning of America's fine navy. Aboard the U.S. Frigate *Constellation*, Captain Thomas Truxtum captured a French frigate. Then, in heavy, storm-ridden seas, against superior gunpower, he defeated another French frigate in a furious battle. The upstart American nation had spunk, determination, punch! Before the young country decided to aid the British, France was glad to wriggle out of the X-Y-Z affair.

At the height of the angry war talk Congress passed and Adams signed the Alien and Sedition Acts. At the sole discretion of the President aliens could be banished from the country and editors could be jailed for "scandalous or malicious" writing against the President or Congress. Obviously these acts abolished freedom of speech and press. The people protested loudly and Southern Republicans, led by Jefferson, adopted resolutions declaring that a state had the right to "nullify" a law believed unconstitutional. Thus an extremely dangerous word entered American thought. And the Alien and Sedition Acts, like the Whisky Rebellion, cemented the will of the people not to stand in awe of leaders like John Adams who believed only the "well-born" should run the government. A revolution didn't have to be fought with bullets alone among free men. It could also be fought with ballots!

In the last troubled months of a stormy Presidency, Adams moved his family into the new White House. Abigail Adams hung her wash to dry in the unfinished East Room and spoke bitterly of the poor presidential mansion the nation had provided. President Adams had another complaint—he couldn't trust his own Cabinet! Hamilton still plotted to unseat him in the next election and this time the Federalists lost the whole game to Jefferson and Aaron Burr.

Adams's last act as President was to appoint John Marshall Chief Justice of the Supreme Court, a happy decision since Marshall's leadership gave the nation a strong legal system. Then, in almost childish rage, Adams left Washington without witnessing Jefferson's inauguration, a bit of foolishness he later regretted.

Adams lived his remaining years in Braintree. Once, reviewing the events of his life, he said:

"I desire no other inscription on my gravestone than this: Here lies John Adams, who took upon himself the responsibility of peace with France in the year 1800." Appropriately this great patriot died on the birthday of American Independence—July 4, 1826.

THOMAS JEFFERSON

"The Art of Being Honest"

IN 1765, about the time John Adams stomped along a street in Braintree filled with scowlish anger over the Stamp Act, a tall, thin youth with carrot-red hair and intense hazel-gray eyes swept like a whirlwind down Duke of Gloucester Street in Williamsburg. Tom Jefferson's destination was the Capitol, where Patrick Henry was denouncing taxation without the consent of the people. On this day the Revolution began in the hearts and minds of many Virginians.

And how did Tom Jefferson feel that day? Excited. Eager. Unafraid.

From almost the moment Tom Jefferson reached Williamsburg to attend the College of William and Mary he had been marked as a bold lad with a future. Within two years, sometimes studying sixteen hours a day, he finished his college courses. If you took a question mark and straightened it into a thin line, you had Tom Jefferson, more or less. Maybe he *did* look like a beanpole that had sprouted arms and legs, but more intellectual curiosity never had been crammed into one person.

And that was why shrewd old George Wythe, whose name rhymed with "Smith," accepted Tom as a law student. Wythe picked his pupils carefully, worked them like slaves, and saw them become great leaders. Jefferson was only one of Wythe's proud products. Another was John Marshall, the fourth Chief Justice of the Supreme Court. Still another was Henry Clay, who became Abe Lincoln's idol.

In a way, Wythe liked Jefferson best. There was spirit, gumption, vitality in this human carrot-top. It wasn't any wonder, really, that he was destined to become a sort of hinge in American history between the bluebloods and the people. By birth he was as aristocratic as any Virginian, and in mind and heart he was as free and independent as any frontiersman in a coonskin cap.

This open-mindedness kept growing in Tom Jefferson as the trait that made him Tom Jefferson—a leader in his own right, his own way. As a young lawyer he would fight for the freedom of a mulatto boy whose parents were slaves, and though he lost the case under an interpretation of law that made slavery perpetual, he didn't lose within himself the belief that all people enjoyed certain God-given rights. As a member of the House of Burgesses, there was a sense of decency and tolerance in the fellow whether he supported legislation to end the ugly sport of cock-fighting or opposed the humiliating ducking of gossipy women in the public pond.

Jefferson's leadership in the struggle to curb the king's repeated abuse of the rights of free-born Englishmen was firm, aggressive, brilliant. No one had to ask him twice to meetings of protest and usually he prodded others to attend. From his pen came a pamphlet entitled "A Summary View of the Rights of British America" that made him famous in England and America. One sentence in that pamphlet expressed his basic faith:

"The whole art of government consists in the art of being honest."

So it was no accident that Jefferson was selected to draft the Declaration of Independence. All through the humid spring of 1776, while the

Continental Congress waited, he worked on this great document. Some said afterward that the ideas he expressed were not new, but one could make the same criticism of the ideas in Lincoln's Gettysburg Address. The point was that Jefferson's mind and spirit touched those ideas and a kind of magic resulted. They became rich, vigorous, brave, enduring. After three days of debate, Congress could find little more than a word or occasional phrase to change in what Jefferson had written. Certainly no one wanted to change this thought:

"We hold these truths to be self-evident: that all men are created equal, that they are endowed by their Creator with certain inalienable rights, that among these are life, liberty and the pursuit of happiness..."

Or to change this thought:

"Governments are instituted among men, deriving their just powers from the consent of the governed."

Jefferson's Declaration of Independence was the climactic victory in the Revolution fought in American hearts and minds as Yorktown was the climactic victory in the shooting war that followed. During those troubled years of conflict Jefferson was twice elected Governor of Virginia, and when the British invaded the Old Dominion State, he escaped capture in a dash on horseback. Later he served as a member of Congress, as Minister to France, as Secretary of State in Washington's Cabinet, and as Vice-President under John Adams.

There seemed to exist little love between Adams, who detested the French Revolution, and Jefferson, who sympathized with it as a popular uprising similar to America's struggle for independence. Even less love existed between Jefferson and Alexander Hamilton. Jefferson believed in the goodness of human nature, and wore plain clothes as a symbol of his faith in the people and democracy, and pleaded for the United States to remain "a nation of farmers." In contrast Hamilton was the silk-stockinged aristocrat who trusted human nature about as much as a rattlesnake, who believed the privileged class should rule, and who argued that only through encouraging shipping and creating manufactures could the country grow strong and prosperous.

Both Jefferson and Hamilton used politics as an ax and, treating the country like a log, split it down the middle while each grabbed a war club. Jefferson's supporters, the Republicans, were chiefly small farmers, frontiersmen and northern mechanics and craftsmen. Hamilton's followers, the Federalists, were largely financiers, merchants and wealthy planters. Hamilton's trouble was that he wanted his political war club to flatten Jefferson and also knock Adams out of power with the Federalists. In 1800 Adams came within three electoral votes of losing the Presidency through Hamilton's wild swinging to and fro, and in 1804, with Hamilton up to the same trick, Jefferson won.

That is, Jefferson didn't lose. The electors intended that Jefferson should be President and Aaron Burr Vice-President, but each elector cast his ballot for the same two men and the vote ended 74 to 74! Thus the selection of President, under the Constitution, was thrown into the House of Representatives, which the Federalists controlled. After thirty-five ballots Jefferson still lacked one of the nine states necessary for election, for Vermont and Maryland refused to break their tie vote.

Unruly mobs roamed the streets of Washington, demanding Jefferson's election as the people's candidate. Hamilton searched his heart. He had fought Tom Jefferson tooth and nail, but he knew that a more honest man had never lived. Could he say as much for Burr? Hamilton's answer was to write endless letters urging Federalists to support Jefferson. On the thirty-sixth ballot Vermont and Maryland switched to the Virginian. From Maine to Florida, as the news of Jefferson's victory spread, people closed their shops to dance and cheer.

Actually the country needed the talents, ideas, genius and fundamental honesty of both Hamilton and Jefferson. In his heart Jefferson knew that and in his inaugural address said: "Every difference of opinion is not difference of principle . . . We are all Republicans—we are all

Federalists." And the policies that Jefferson practiced as President were not much different from what the country would have expected under a Federalist. A strict economy in governmental expenditures reduced the national debt and lowered taxes. The end of the excise tax on whisky makers certainly lost Jefferson no votes among back-country farmers. In a stiff little war with Tripoli the small but proud United States Navy stopped the Barbary pirates from preying on American ships.

The nation's capital grew used to Jefferson's odd habits. The British Ambassador, wearing a splendid uniform and a dress sword, became indignant when the President received him in a pair of old carpet slippers. Jefferson chuckled. He liked old carpet slippers. They let him wriggle his toes. He could think better.

One event that gave Jefferson considerable reason for thought was Spain's acquisition from France of the Louisiana Territory. A glance at the map showed how vital a seaport New Orleans was to frontier Americans who depended on the old Mississippi to reach the outside world. What Jefferson most feared occurred in 1803. Spain closed the port of New Orleans, then ceded the territory back to France where the warlike Napoleon Bonaparte had gained power.

Jefferson had to do something. He sent his old Virginia friend, James

28

Monroe, to Paris in an effort to buy the island on which New Orleans was located. Napoleon, plotting a war against England, badly needed money. He offered Jefferson "a noble bargain"—the entire Louisiana Territory for $15,000,000!

Jefferson wasn't sure that he had the right, under the Constitution, to make this purchase—but he made it, anyhow! The Senate backed him up by a vote of 26 to 5, and the House by a vote of 90 to 25, so the nervous toe-wriggling inside the old carpet slippers subsided. Then the President authorized Meriwether Lewis and William Clark to explore the territory and tell him whether the country had received its money's worth.

Starting from St. Louis, Lewis and Clark traveled 8,000 miles before reaching Oregon and the Pacific Ocean. The White House soon became a curious place as Jefferson exhibited the gifts the explorers sent him. In the garden stood a cage with live grizzly bears! Stuffed antelopes from the Great Plains, the skeleton of a prairie wolf, clothes worn by the Sioux — with delight Jefferson displayed his prizes. Later arrived furs of the red fox, white hare, marten and yellow bear along with cases containing live prairie hens, magpies and a burrowing squirrel. What a bargain he had bought — over 827,000 square miles along with control of the old Mississippi! Here was a whole new American empire!

Toward the close of Jefferson's first term, Vice-President Aaron Burr became implicated in a reputed plot among northeastern Federalists to break up the Union rather than submit to another four years of Republican rule. Hamilton exposed the plot, a loyal act resulting in the duel with Burr that cost Hamilton his life. As a result Jefferson was overwhelmingly re-elected by an electoral vote of 162 to 14 and every New England state except Connecticut supported him.

Sad days awaited Burr. Captured in 1806 on the Ohio River, he was charged with recruiting forces to further the plot of disunion, and brought to Richmond to stand trial for treason. Chief Justice Marshall acquitted Burr, who fled to Europe, a man perhaps unjustly disgraced.

The Burr trial was only one upsetting episode during Jefferson's second term. England and France, now at war, both recklessly seized neutral ships on the high seas. Then the British frigate *Leopard* fired on the American frigate *Chesapeake* and war threatened. Jefferson, convinced that America was unprepared for an armed conflict, tried to fight with economic measures. He forced through Congress the Embargo Act that all but stopped foreign trade. A furor resulted. Tobacco, wheat and other exports piled up on American docks. Shipbuilders lost their jobs. Massachusetts shippers defied the law by going to sea and people ridiculed the act by spelling it backward: "O-grab-me!" On March 1, 1809 the act was repealed. Jefferson was no longer a popular hero.

Washington had believed that two terms in the Presidency were sufficient for any man, and Jefferson was glad to follow his example. And as public service had kept Washington for long years from enjoying his home at Mount Vernon, so had Jefferson been exiled from his beloved home, Monticello, standing atop a beautiful mountain near Charlottesville, Virginia. Jefferson had designed this magnificent home, and it reflected the genius of his mind which also had compiled a dictionary of Indian dialects, invented a clock that told both the hour and the day of the week, built a plow that won a prize in a French exhibit, and devised the decimal system of dollars and cents used in American currency!

One of the greatest pleasures of Jefferson's final years at Monticello was planning the University of Virginia. He designed its fine buildings, decided what courses should be taught, hired its teachers, and even chose the books for its library. Another happy incident was learning that John Adams had said: "I always loved Jefferson and still love him." The two old patriots and ex-Presidents renewed their friendship. On July 4, 1826 —the fiftieth birthday of the Declaration of Independence—John Adams lay dying in Braintree and so too did Jefferson at Monticello. He was then eighty-three and had given sixty of those years to public service. His breathing stopped but not his spirit. That lives on and on and on.

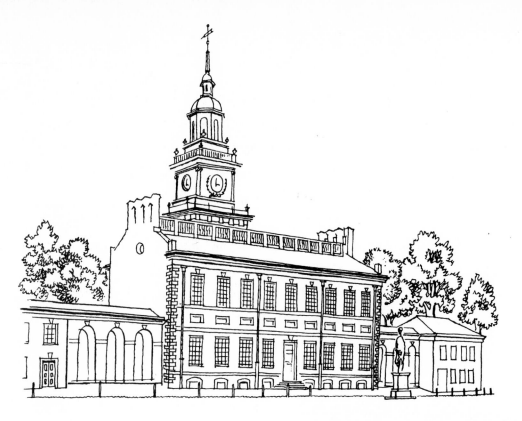

JAMES MADISON

"Father of the Constitution"

PHILADELPHIA throbbed with excitement. Everywhere famous men strolled the streets.

"Look!" cried one Philadelphian. "There's George Washington! A dusty sight he makes, after his long ride from Mount Vernon!"

Everyone recognized Ben Franklin, Philadelphia's own first citizen. When Alexander Hamilton was pointed out, some muttered: "A stiff-necked dandy, by the look of him!"

A frail, quiet-spoken Virginian who often passed unnoticed that May of 1787 was James Madison. Yet when the convention now assembling ended its important work, wise men said: "Madison was the leader. 'Tis he who should be called the Father of the Constitution."

All his life Madison possessed this ability to surprise everyone by accomplishing ten times more than they expected. A sickly child, he was forced to receive his early education from private tutors. Yet at the age of twenty he graduated from the College of New Jersey (now Princeton), and three years later plunged into a vigorous career in politics.

Right from the start, Madison revealed a streak of hardheaded independence.

"Be reasonable," friends begged during one of his first campaigns. "The way to carry an election is to give voters a few free drinks of whisky."

But Madison wouldn't play that game. He lost the election.

Still, sober-thinking Virginians realized that young Madison was a man they needed in government and appointed him to the Governor's Council. Quickly he became distinguished as the father of religious liberty. A clause in Virginia's proposed "bill of rights" stated that all men were entitled to "the fullest toleration" in the exercise of religion.

Madison began asking questions. If a state had a right to "tolerate" religious opinion, could it not also "prohibit" such opinion? What business had a state in claiming *any* jurisdiction over a man's religion? Under Madison's prodding, Virginia changed the clause to read that "all men are equally entitled to the free exercise of religion, according to the dictates of conscience."

The battle didn't end there. Next Virginia attempted to tax the people "for the support of teachers of the Christian religion." Almost alone, Madison fought a law that could be used to establish a state church. At that time nearly every state imposed some form of "religious test" upon civil office-holders, and it was through the abolition of these tests that Madison waged his battle to separate the powers of church and state. In writing, he carried on a one-man crusade—and won!

So the frail, quiet-spoken Virginian who, on mild May evenings in 1787, walked the streets of Philadelphia unnoticed, was respected behind the scenes for his personal charm and courageous, well-informed mind. Already the Constitutional Convention was becoming a battleground for state delegations pushing for their own selfish interests.

Stanley Dersh

Madison asked the right questions. Why had the old Continental Congresses failed to raise revenue, and, in many instances, even to preserve order? Was it not because the members of those Congresses were mere envoys from the states empowered only to deliberate and advise on legislation? Should not Congress represent the people directly?

Cried one set of angry delegates: "What wicked scheme is this to destroy the authority of the states?" Cried another set of angry delegates: "The large states are in league to enslave the small states!"

Madison, who hated public speaking, threw himself into the bitter discussions. With eloquence the congenial, soft-spoken Virginian led the bickerers to a common ground. He quieted fears and answered angry questions. Out of the torrent of words emerged a bold idea of government.

At the core of that idea was the revolutionary decision to divide authority between state and federal governments. To satisfy the small states, each state was to be represented equally in the upper house (Senate) of the Federal Congress and by population in the lower house (House of Representatives).

The southern states, which hitherto had insisted that slaves be recognized as mere chattels, raised a new storm by insisting that slaves be counted in their populations. Madison proposed a compromise. In computing population, he suggested, let five slaves be counted as three persons. Though many delegates found this "three-fifths rule" a bitter pill, they swallowed it so that the southern states would accept the Constitution.

Disturbed and grumbling, the delegates went home. The people must decide now whether to accept or reject the Convention's work. On the bright side no one could deny that by dividing federal authority among the legislative, executive and judicial branches of government the Constitution provided an intelligent system of checks and balances. The fiercest opposition, however, arose from another quarter. North and south, rasping voices shouted: "Where is the 'bill of rights'? You do not protect the liberties of the individual!"

Madison plunged into the fight to save the Constitution for which he had been so largely responsible. With Alexander Hamilton and John Jay, he wrote *The Federalist Papers* that defended with brilliant arguments the new form of government. In Virginia he beat down opposition under the leadership of Patrick Henry and saw his state ratify the Constitution by the close legislative vote of 89 to 79. Later, as a member of the first United States Congress, he offered twelve amendments to the Constitution and had ten accepted as the "Bill of Rights" guaranteeing to every American—

Freedom of religion, of speech, of the press, and of assembly.

The right to petition the government.

Fair arrest and fair trial with protection against cruel and unusual punishment.

The right to bear arms.

Through all of Madison's long and busy career, he would achieve no more important work than in his role as "Father of the Constitution." And Madison surely was busy in later years, first as Jefferson's chief lieutenant in the political war between the Republicans and Hamilton's Federalists, and then as Secretary of State during the eight years that Jefferson was President.

As Jefferson's successor in the Presidency, Madison stepped into the hornets' nest of a possible war with England or France. In Congress now appeared a new kind of personality—the go-ahead Westerners, of whom Henry Clay of Kentucky was the leader. These "war hawks" had their eyes on the annexation of Canada and Spanish Florida.

Madison was for peace and tried to play England against France by declaring that if one would stop attacking American commerce at sea, the United States would break off commercial relations with the other. The wily Napoleon, without any intention of keeping his word, agreed to Madison's terms. The "war hawks" shouted louder than ever for war and Madison finally appealed to Congress to declare war on England without knowing that twenty-four hours earlier the British Government had voted to stop its abuses against American ships and sailors.

So the War of 1812 was our most unnecessary war. Still, both on land and sea it was bitterly fought, and two heroes of its battlefields, Andrew Jackson and William Henry Harrison, later became President. Madison saw with his own eyes the devastation of that war when the British captured the city of Washington in the summer of 1814. Beautiful Dolly Madison, the President's wife, escaped a step ahead of the invaders, carrying silver, important papers and other valuables. The Madisons returned to find only the blackened walls of the White House.

What the War of 1812 accomplished was all indirect. New England Federalists, opposed to the war, met secretly in Hartford late in 1814 and so convinced the country that they were embarked on some traitorous scheme that Madison was assured of re-election. Watching British ships shelling Baltimore's Fort McHenry, Francis Scott Key was inspired to write "The Star-Spangled Banner." And whereas we gained none of the territory that the "war hawks" coveted, we proved to the world that the American army and navy were tough fighting organizations.

But the greatest gain from the War of 1812 was the sense it gave us of being a nation. Suddenly we were more confident of our future and we entered pleasant, productive years that became known as "the era of good feeling." In 1816 we passed the first tariff to protect industries and that same year Indiana was admitted as a state. We read the writings of William Cullen Bryant, James Fenimore Cooper and Washington Irving and liked the American tone of these works. As a people, we had something to say, something to give to the world.

Madison's eight years in the Presidency ended on this happy note in 1817 and he returned to his beautiful home, Montpelier, in Orange County, Virginia, to outlive all the other founders of the American Republic. The frail, sickly child, who always surprised his neighbors, lived to be eighty-five when on a June day in 1836, death claimed him.

JAMES MONROE

"America for Americans"

"LIEUTENANT, you've fought in a lot of this war. What think ye of this scheme to take Trenton?"

James Monroe smiled. He was eighteen now. In a way, he *had* been in a lot of the war since those days earlier in the year when along with twenty-five of the thirty students at William and Mary he had quit college to fight with Washington. He had heard cannon rumble and bullets whistle at the battles of Harlem and White Plains. He had seen men die —no pleasant sight. He had charged with fixed bayonet, hearing men cursing and moaning around him. Sometimes he thought that these battles were only part of a fight that had been gathering strength since he was a child of seven and the Stamp Act had unloosed the first angry outbursts against the British. In late December of 1776, eleven years later, the torrent of words had become a torrent of bullets.

"Lieutenant, has fear paralyzed your tongue?" Colonel Glover asked.

"No," Monroe answered. "I'll do my part as well as you'll do yours."

"Meaning what, sir?"

Monroe chuckled. "That I'll do it well. After all, when General Washington decided that your men should handle the boats in crossing the river, could he have decided more wisely?"

"You mean, could he find better boatmen than those Massachusetts fishermen from Marblehead? No better exist, sir!"

The Hessians held Trenton and Washington gambled that an old dog couldn't be taught new tricks. Christmas in Germany was a time for dancing and beer-drinking—a great deal of beer-drinking. And what made a man sleepier than a belly full of beer? Could there be a better moment to surprise those Hessians than on the morning after Christmas?

On Christmas night Washington marched his troops to the Delaware River. A snowstorm filled the cold, raw night, and some soldiers wrapped rags around their feet while others trudged along barefoot. Yet none complained—this fact Monroe always remembered. And he remembered also the sight of Washington, bundled in his cloak, standing on the bank of the river, calm and collected, with the snow turning to sleet and cutting like a knife. By daylight the army was across the river and Monroe led part of the forces that must overpower the Hessian guards.

He waited tensely. Drums beat. A bugle sounded. From the west came the boom of cannon. The Americans swept forward—men running, officers swinging their swords, artillerymen harnessing their horses.

Monroe rolled his troops down the Princeton Road. The Hessians came out with muskets flashing. Monroe felt a sting in his shoulder, but ignored the wound. The surprise had worked. The American charge carried forward as though it were storm-driven, and the Hessians threw down their guns. In the story of this war one of its brightest chapters now must be entitled "Trenton."

And Monroe had been in the thick of it, as afterward he was in the thick of the fighting at Brandywine, Germantown and Monmouth. He rose in rank to lieutenant colonel. Sent to collect information in regard to the prospects and conditions of the southern army, he chafed at being shunted away from the excitement of battle. But the one event of the war that would affect most his later life occurred now. He made a new and warm friend of Virginia's Governor, Thomas Jefferson.

First as a member of the Virginia Assembly, then for three terms as a member of the Continental Congress, Monroe became a stanch advocate of a national policy guaranteeing to the people of the West the right to free navigation of the Mississippi River. Twice he journeyed across the Alleghenies to learn at first hand the nature of the western country.

The debate over the ratification of the Constitution found Monroe siding with the opposition led by Patrick Henry. Monroe feared the new form of government for two reasons. Would not constant conflict result between state and the federal authority? And what was to stop a president from remaining in office for life? The answers came from the quiet-spoken Madison, and Monroe was won over, though he surrendered grudgingly and never quite lost either fear.

Like all the "Virginia dynasts" who became President, Monroe quickly fell out with Hamilton. Washington's policy as President was to keep both factions happy and so he appointed John Jay, the Federalist, Minister to England and James Monroe, the Republican, envoy to France. Monroe reached Paris in the turmoil of the French Revolution. He handled himself well, considering the circumstances, but he was criticized severely at home and then recalled.

Monroe bided his time. Like Jefferson, he had become one of the favorites of the anti-Federalists, who elected him Governor of Virginia. When Jefferson became President, Monroe and Robert R. Livingston went to France to negotiate the Louisiana Purchase.

"We have lived long, but this is the noblest work of our lives," Livingston told Monroe.

Napoleon Bonaparte offered Monroe another lesson in international politics. The French emperor needed money badly, but when he thought of what this vast territory could mean to the young American nation, he made no secret of what else he had accomplished: "I have given to England a maritime rival that will sooner or later humble her pride!"

Appointment as Minister to England and Spain, another term in the Virginia Assembly, and election for the second time as Governor of Virginia filled Monroe's busy career until the election of Madison as President. Called into the Cabinet, Monroe served for six years as Secretary of State and from 1814-15 also as Secretary of War. By the time Madison's second term ended, Monroe had held almost every important office except that of President and he became the logical Republican candidate to oppose Rufus King, the Federalist nominee. Monroe won easily by an electoral vote of 183 to 34.

The nation relaxed in a sunny "era of good feeling." During the eight years that Monroe served as President (only one electoral vote was cast against him in 1821), Florida was acquired from Spain, a border settlement was reached between Canada and the United States, the Santa Fe Trail opened, the first public high school was established, and five new states were admitted (Mississippi, Illinois, Alabama, Maine, Missouri).

More and more the nation was like a boy growing into manhood, feeling the strength in its own muscles, hearing the call to adventure across mountains and plains, and believing implicitly in "America for Americans." Yet trouble was brewing. When Missouri was carved out of the territory acquired through the Louisiana Purchase, slavery already existed there and it was expected that Missouri would be admitted as a slave state.

All at once the lid blew off an easy-going nation. Congress seethed with hot tempers. The twenty-two states that then composed the Union were evenly divided—eleven slave states, eleven free. True, this balance had been broken previously, but always on a geographical basis that kept slavery contained east of the Mississippi River within the boundaries of the Mason and Dixon Line and the Ohio River.

If Missouri were admitted at all, thundered some Northerners, it must be without slavery. What right, snapped Southerners, did Congress have to interfere with private property? The Missouri Compromise admitted Maine as a free state and Missouri as a slave state, thus maintaining the balance. In all territory resulting from the Louisiana Purchase, the southern boundary of Missouri along the line of 36° 30′ north latitude was extended as the dividing line between slave-soil and free-soil. An uneasy peace had been won. With outward politeness, North and South buried their hatchets. But each knew the spot of burial.

Monroe took little part in the Missouri Compromise. His name would live in American history for a much quieter event. On December 2, 1823 he sent his annual message to Congress. One paragraph announced that a letter had been sent to the governments of Russia and England, informing them that the American continents were not subject to future colonization by any European power.

A second paragraph said that should an attempt at colonization be made, the United States would consider its own peace and safety endangered. Specifically for the eyes of Portugal and Spain, the message declared that if any European power interfered with the independence of governments in North and South America, such interference would be regarded as an unfriendly act.

The Monroe Doctrine was a tremendous announcement. It said, bluntly, that henceforth all American countries belonged to North and South Americans. And young though we still were, we stood with our foot against the door for future colonizers and aggressors. To the rest of the world we said: "Take heed."

The world did. Today the Monroe Doctrine is as vital a force in international affairs as it was on July 4, 1831 when its author died in New York City. James Monroe was then past seventy-three, and not one of his years had been wasted since, as a young lieutenant of eighteen, he had charged down on the Hessians at Trenton.

JOHN QUINCY ADAMS
"Our Most Independent President"

LIKE a good son, John Quincy Adams always obeyed his father and mother and it was their wish that one day he should be President of the United States.

Other early Presidents became patriots in the cause of American independence, but John Quincy Adams was born a patriot. As a child, holding his mother's hand, he watched the flashing guns as British and Continental troops fought the Battle of Bunker Hill. His warm boyhood friends and advisors included George Washington, Benjamin Franklin and Thomas Jefferson. By the time he was eighteen, accompanying his distinguished father on diplomatic missions, he had traveled to France, Holland, Russia, England, Denmark, Sweden and Germany.

He returned to America to do what was expected of any good Adams —to graduate from Harvard. No one who knew John Quincy Adams ever doubted that he would live up to the traditions of his famous family.

All Adamses possessed, as a matter of nature, bright minds, frugal habits and independent spirits. John Quincy Adams really beat the whole Adams clan in this last trait. He could be as stubborn as a hundred mules.

Like his great father, John Quincy Adams studied law after Harvard, but he didn't enjoy legal work. In his spare time, using such pen names as "Publicola" and "Columbus," he wrote articles defending President Washington's policies or attacking Thomas Paine's "dangerous" ideas about the natural rights of the common man. Usually his father was believed to have written these articles, but this mistake didn't bother John Quincy Adams. He received the credit where it counted—from President Washington, for example, who in 1794 appointed him Minister to Holland and two years later Minister to Portugal.

When Jefferson became President the diplomatic career of any Federalist who was also an Adams was doomed to end, at least temporarily. Strong-minded John Quincy Adams came home to serve in the Massachusetts Legislature and then in the United States Senate. He could not escape very easily the bitter political feud between his father and Hamilton, and the viciousness of that quarrel might have broken a less independent spirit.

Hamilton's Federalists teamed up with the Republicans to insult young Adams at every opportunity. Any motion he offered was at once voted down and then, introduced again by one of his enemies, often was passed! John Quincy Adams tightened his mouth. If the Federalists wanted a fight, they were knocking at the right door! So when most Federalists opposed Jefferson's Louisiana Purchase, young Adams supported it. Even though both England and France were playing the bully in seizing American ships and sailors on the high seas, most Federalists hated Britain to the point where they would stand any French insult as long as they could strike back at the British—but not John Quincy Adams! He supported Jefferson's embargo against both countries and seemed to thrive on the abuse Federalists heaped upon him.

Stanley Dersh

About all the Federalists accomplished was to make young Adams acceptable to the Republicans, and almost President Madison's first act was to appoint John Quincy Adams Minister to Russia. Later he was one of the three American commissioners who negotiated the treaty ending the War of 1812, and then was named Minister to England.

History had indeed repeated itself! Old John Adams had negotiated the treaty with England at the close of the Revolutionary War before being named Ambassador to the Court of St. James, and now his son, performing the same role in negotiating the treaty after a second war with England, had been similarly honored!

Under President Monroe, John Quincy Adams became a distinguished Secretary of State. His greatest achievement was the treaty whereby Spain ceded Florida to the United States. The same treaty also established the boundary between Mexico and Louisiana along the Sabine and Red rivers, the upper Arkansas, the crest of the Rocky Mountains and the 42nd parallel. A stanch belief in independence—the one characteristic that best described John Quincy Adams — made him an avid supporter of a policy recognizing the governments of colonies that had revolted against Spain in South America. Informed sources in Washington knew that he was the principal author of the famous Monroe Doctrine.

As Monroe's second term drew to an end, the obvious candidates to succeed him numbered five: John Quincy Adams; William H. Crawford, Secretary of the Treasury; John C. Calhoun, Secretary of War (who later withdrew); Henry Clay, Speaker of the House; and Andrew Jackson, the nation's military hero.

No one really wanted John Quincy Adams, except perhaps a handful of loyal New Englanders. Adams's manner was stiff and often downright unpleasant. His remarks could be disagreeably blunt. He didn't care if he made a friend or lost one. Asked what he intended to do in helping his own chances for election, he answered growlishly:

"Absolutely nothing!"

Calhoun easily won the Vice-Presidency, but the electoral vote for President stood: 90 for Jackson, 84 for Adams, 41 for Crawford, 37 for Clay. The election now went to the House of Representatives. Clay, throwing his support behind Adams, assured victory for the New Englander, who appointed Clay his Secretary of State. Jackson charged that he had been beaten by a deal between "the Puritan and the black-leg." The charge was untrue, but no one ever convinced Jackson of Adams's innocence.

Adams served but one term as President, and had precious little to show for it. Elsewhere America moved ahead—the Erie Canal was completed in 1825, the American labor movement began in 1827, and Webster published his dictionary in 1828 — but the best that Adams seemed capable of achieving in Washington was chaos. Congress bitterly thwarted his pet plans to build Federal highways, canals, a national university and Federal weather stations.

At the root of the dissension was the fact that the country was breaking up into new political factions. The Whigs favored Adams's internal improvements, a national bank and high tariff, whereas the Democrats under Jackson opposed these measures as unconstitutional.

As usual John Quincy Adams became a problem to his own supporters, and especially to those who argued: "To the victor belongs the spoils." Adams sniffed at a "spoils system" that demanded a good man be removed from public office because he belonged to a different political party. He asked for no favors—he would give none! Meanwhile Jackson's popularity skyrocketed. To nobody's great surprise he defeated Adams in the election of 1828.

The only decent course for a defeated President—or so claimed the critics of John Quincy Adams—was to go home and mind his own business. But what Adams ever had to be told what to do? Let his enemies cry that it was undignified for a former President to seek election to Congress—let them, in effect, waste their breath if that gave them any

pleasure! In 1831 Adams returned to the rough-and-tumble quarrels of Congress, and there he remained until his death in 1848.

After all, he had obeyed papa and mama—he had been President —and now he would do as he wished. He became even more ruggedly independent, refusing to be bound by any political party, supporting Jackson when he believed the President right and attacking him unmercifully when their opinions differed. Adams saw himself as the Elder Statesman, as "the man of the whole nation." Others might tremble for their political futures if they took an active part in the rising dispute over slavery, but he dove headlong into this political hornets' nest.

In those days the only method by which opponents of the "peculiar institution" could present their case to Congress was through offering petitions for the abolition of slavery in the District of Columbia. In 1836 pro-slavery forces in Congress proposed a "gag-rule" to prohibit either the discussion or publication of such petitions. John Quincy Adams rose to his feet. His voice was firm and resounding, his position unshakable:

"I hold the resolution to be a direct violation of the Constitution of the United States, the rules of this house, and the rights of my constituents!"

With loud shrieks and yells of "Order! Order!" Adams's foes tried vainly to drown out his words. By a vote of 117 to 68 the "gag-rule" passed.

But John Quincy Adams, who loved a one-man fight, was far from defeated. In every session of Congress he renewed the quarrel. He proved a master at debate and his strong voice fell upon his opponents like a volley of cannon. Threatened with assassination, he seemed to grow in the force of his attacks.

Suddenly Adams stood before the nation as a bulwark of strength around which opponents of slavery could rally. They came to love and even to idolize this unbending old man. And gradually his enemies began to reveal a grudging respect for the dauntless, quick-witted, thoroughly cussed old warrior. In 1845 came his great triumph—Congress rescinded the "gag-rule."

The nine-year struggle over the "gag-rule" foreshadowed much more than many realized. What would happen if ever a war involved the slave-holding interests? "I say," Adams warned, "that the military authority takes for the time the place of all municipal institutions, slavery among the rest." The date of this utterance was April 14, 1842—more than twenty years before President Lincoln, using the same argument, issued the Emancipation Proclamation!

In November, 1846, a stroke kept John Quincy Adams at home for four months. He had returned to Congress, and was occupying his seat, when on February 21, 1848 a second stroke occurred. Friends carried him to the speaker's chamber, where he lay for two days.

"This is the last of earth," he said finally. "I am content."

Gently breath left the body of "our most independent President."

ANDREW JACKSON

"Old Hickory"

FOR FORTY YEARS Virginians and the Adams family of Massachusetts had monopolized the Presidency. But America was no longer a tight little nation of states stretched along the Atlantic seacoast. The country was big and sprawling now—and growing bigger and more sprawling every year. A new spirit was rising, a kind of rough-and-ready freedom that said, "For two cents, I'd poke your nose." Out of this new America came our seventh President—two-fisted Andrew Jackson, who helped to teach Sam Houston and Davy Crockett how to fight.

"Yip, yip, yip, hoo-ray for Old Hickory," shouted frontiersmen when they saw Jackson. Andy was their idol. He was one of them, a coonskin kinsman!

In a log cabin in Waxhaw settlement on the border between North and South Carolina, Jackson was born on March 15, 1767. A few days after Andy's birth his father died, so life started cruelly for him. What

50

little education he received was in an "old-field school"—principally the three R's—and even then Andy never really conquered the "'ritin'" part.

After the fall of Charleston in 1780, the British overran South Carolina. Thirteen-year-old Andy, whose mother and two brothers would die from hardships suffered in the Revolutionary War, was grabbed by the Redcoats and carried to Camden. He nearly starved in prison. He refused to clean the boots of a British officer and that ugly fellow, striking Andy with his sword, cut the lad's arm to the bone. In his heart Andy stored up a grudge against the British that he meant to pay back double whenever he got the chance.

Alone in the world, young Jackson was apprenticed for a time to a saddler and at the age of eighteen began the study of law. He was no saint, and one neighbor described him as "the most roaring, rollicking, game-cocking, horse-racing, card-playing, mischievous fellow" in those parts. As a frontier lawyer, his legal knowledge was small but his friends were many. That combination was a good one.

So Andy traveled in the emigrant train to Nashville, where on Court Days he fitted like a pea in a pod. Men came to town mainly to talk politics, drink whisky and fight, and Andy could always hold his own in that sort of company. Maybe Andy was a diamond in the rough by the Adams standard, and too ready with a pistol for a polished Virginian, but around Nashville in those years when the Indians averaged one murder every ten days, a man lived by his wits.

Andy went ahead fast. In 1796 he was in Knoxville, helping to write a constitution for Tennessee, and witnesses said afterward that he had wanted to name the new state "Great Crooked River." He went to Washington to serve a term in the House of Representatives and another in the Senate, resigning that office to become a judge in Tennessee's supreme court. He was always in a scrap of some sort—over his wife whom he married before her divorce became legal, or in court, or trying to pay his debts, or dueling over some insult, or defending Aaron Burr against the charge

51

of treason—and yet his popularity increased, no matter how deeply he waded into trouble.

The War of 1812 gave Andy a chance to settle that old grudge against the British, and also to whack some sense into the hated Indians. No one could wear him down on a march, and admiring his sturdiness, men called him, affectionately, "Old Hickory." At Fort Minns on the shore of Lake Tensaw in the southern part of what is now Alabama, August 30, 1813 was a day of horror. Creek warriors, under the half-breed chief, Weathersford, howled out of the forests and left behind four hundred murdered men, women and children.

Andy led the 2,500 militiamen—among them Sam Houston and Davy Crockett—who set out, grimly resolved to put an end to these bloodthirsty Creeks. Wilderness marching was no lark. Often the men were hungry for days, and mutiny grows in empty bellies. Now Andy showed his superb military leadership, even though at times he had one half of his army keeping the other half from going home. In a bloody battle on the Horseshoe Bend of the Tallapoosa River, Andy hit the Creeks so hard and furiously that there was never much fight in them afterward. Many wanted to hang Weathersford, but Andy spared the chief's life, and the friendship that ripened thereafter between the Creeks and the settlers proved him to be a shrewd wilderness diplomat.

Andy settled next his grudge against the British. He was now a major general in the regular army with command of the entire Department of the South. What made military sense in the wilderness did not always seem clear to the War Department in Washington, but as they said in those days, Andy never hesitated "to act upon the necessity." The British were using Spanish Florida as a base, and Andy, acting on his own, went in and drove them out. Federalist newspapers blasted Andy's high-handedness, but quite sensibly Andy pushed on to deal with the British in New Orleans.

The British marched on this vital seaport with 12,000 fine troops

under Sir Edward Pakenham, brother-in-law of the celebrated Iron Duke of Wellington. Andy's own forces numbered about half that number, but Andy knew that his boys could fight equally well with a rifle, knife or tomahawk, and he did not mistake his great luck when Sir Edward made a fatal military blunder by launching simultaneous assaults with two widely separated forces. Andy realized that he had the British then—and had them good.

"Boys," he told his backwoodsmen-soldiers, "don't get too anxious to fire those rifles. Wait till you have 'em in range, then give it to 'em just above the breastplates."

"Right," answered grinning Tennesseeans and Kentuckians.

Pakenham's troops came on, in neat rows, and the cry ran along the American line: "Go to it, boys—pick 'em off!"

There was never a battle quite like it. British troops dropped like flies being swatted. Pakenham counted 700 killed, 1,400 wounded, 500 captured. Andy's losses were 8 killed, 13 wounded!

With the War of 1812 ending at New Orleans, the treacherous situation in Spanish Florida could no longer be ignored. Renegade Indians and runaway Negroes had banded into mobs of raiders and murderers. Spain, occupied with colonies in revolt in South America, paid little heed to how pirates were turning Florida into a cutthroat's haven. Fifty white men, ascending the Appalachicola River, were set upon by Indians, tortured with firebrands, and then massacred, a slaughter that was only one example of many depredations. Orders reached General Jackson to proceed to the frontier.

The orders were not clear. Andy honestly believed that his instructions were to take possession of Florida on the ground that Spain could not control it. Within three months he restored order. Among his prisoners were a Scotch trader named Alexander Arbuthnot and a young English lieutenant named Robert Ambrister. Andy believed both were guilty of inciting the Indians. He shot Ambrister and hanged Arbuthnot.

"My God would not have smiled on me, had I punished only the poor ignorant savages, and spared the white men who set them on," declared Andy when severe criticism greeted these hasty executions.

Nor did Andy explain how the country was to wriggle out of the delicate diplomatic situation he had created. A future political enemy, John Quincy Adams, managed that neat maneuver for him!

Andy was unchangeable. He was rough, tough, emotional and headstrong. An idea planted in his mind, whether right or wrong, stuck there like a porcupine's quill. He was always quarreling with someone—and finding that the people loved his spunk and sassiness. He believed to his dying breath that had it not been for the trickery of Adams and Clay, "the Puritan and the blackleg," he would have been elected President in 1824. Four years later he defeated Adams easily by an electoral vote of 178 to 83.

So America had its first western President—and, in character, Jackson proved to be a stormy one. He possessed no qualms about applying the "spoils system." In forty years previously the total number of men removed from public office had been 74, but in one year Jackson ousted 2,000 workers from civil service. Chivalry toward women was one of Jackson's finest traits, and attacks upon the reputation of the wife of his Secretary of War found Jackson scornful of such gossip. When his Cabinet resigned, he coolly appointed another. A little group of intimate friends, who thought sensibly about the "spoils system" and hated Adams and Clay, became the principal advisors in his secret and somewhat unsavory "kitchen cabinet."

Two great national problems plunged Jackson hip-deep into trouble. He could not be blamed, of course, for the tariff of 1828—called properly the "tariff of abominations"—that had discriminated with rank unfairness against the South. During Jackson's first term that dangerous word, "nullification," often was heard, if only as a surly mutter. Then the tariff of 1832, failing to remove many levies that Southerners found most objectionable, produced the explosion.

Jackson's mouth twitched angrily as he read reports of the action taken by South Carolina on November 19, 1832. Both the tariffs of 1828 and 1832, decided a South Carolina convention, were "null and void"—meaning, specifically, that they were not to be obeyed. And the South Carolinians served warning on the Federal Government. Should any effort be made to enforce these revenue laws, South Carolina would secede from the Union!

Once at a dinner in Washington the President had proposed a toast: "The Federal Union—it must be preserved." In Andy, South Carolina was dealing with the son of a frontier where questioning a man's word was a dangerous enterprise for anyone unprepared to shoot fast and straight. And Andy prepared to fight, sending a naval force under Lieutenant David Farragut to Charleston Harbor and ordering General Winfield Scott to stand ready to march troops into South Carolina.

The people of the country—even a large number of southern people—clearly supported Jackson's get-tough policy. South Carolina backed down. So once again the nation's skies darkened, the thunder rumbled, and then the gathering storm was swept away. Yet thoughtful minds uneasily counted up the accumulating signs of the threatening tempest—the Missouri Compromise, nullification in South Carolina, the pro-slavery forces aligned against the Free-soilers, John Quincy Adams's one-man war on the "gag-rule."

In the banking crisis, Jackson failed miserably. People ignorant of the nature of money and trade easily respond to attacks on capitalists and corporations, and yet it was unfair to call Jackson a demagogue in this respect since on the subject of money and banking he was almost as ignorant as anyone. No one could dispute that there had been some mismanagement of the national bank, but Jackson, who habitually believed the worst of whatever he opposed, exaggerated the case. Moreover, Clay supported the national bank—evidence to Jackson and his "kitchen cabinet" that this institution must be the tool of the devil.

Attempts to curtail the President's veto power and to restrict his right to make appointments merely strengthened Jackson's fierce, combative spirit and made him appear more and more the beleaguered "champion of the people" fighting the evil money interests. So Jackson won his campaign to deposit public funds in state banks, which soon were ridiculed as Jackson's "pet banks." Paper money flooded the country and prices shot upward under a wave of reckless speculation.

That circumstance was all the more unfortunate since, during Jackson's Presidency, America enjoyed a remarkable period of growth. Railroads and ocean navigation expanded. Arkansas and Michigan joined the Union and Texas won its independence. Cyrus McCormick invented the harvester and the Erie and Champlain Canals were joined to extend our internal waterway. Friction matches were invented, the first penny newspaper published, and a young city called Chicago began growing like a weed on the shores of Lake Michigan. Then the Panic of 1837 crashed down upon the country. Thousands of private fortunes were scattered to the winds, along with a good share of Jackson's personal popularity.

Jackson returned to Nashville to spend his remaining years in his beautiful home, The Hermitage, where he died on June 8, 1845. The country could not forget rough-hewn Andy. With all his faults, he remained a symbol of towering strength, courage and unflinching devotion to the Union. For these virtues he would be endeared forever to his countrymen as "Old Hickory."

MARTIN VAN BUREN

"The Red Fox of Kinderhook"

JACKSON picked Martin Van Buren as his successor in the Presidency. Those who watched the dapper Van Buren strolling the streets of Washington must have blinked their eyes. On a Sunday, bound for church, the President might appear dressed in a snuff-colored coat, orange cravat, pearl-shaded vest, white duck trousers and morocco shoes.

The President's elegance emphasized the capital's drab appearance. Washington now was a city of about 40,000 inhabitants. Pigs rooted in its muddy roads and chickens fluttered along its paths. Open sewers spread their stench and disease everywhere.

And how had a dandy like Van Buren ascended to the princely position of master in this mudhole? Jackson had backed him—everyone knew that. They knew also that the President's home was in Kinderhook, New York, and since his political backers had organized the Old Kinderhook Club, if you supported Van Buren you were "O.K."—a new expression in the American language. Under Jackson, Van Buren had served as Secretary of State, Minister to England and Vice-President—and his friends called him "Little Van" or the "Little Magician," and those not so friendly referred to him as "The Red Fox of Kinderhook." He was unique as the first President who had not been born a British subject.

Actually Martin Van Buren owed no apology for his high position. Born in Kinderhook on December 5, 1782, the son of a thrifty Dutch tavern keeper, Martin had begun the study of law at the age of fourteen and two years later had tried—and won—his first lawsuit!

Successively Van Buren served in the State Senate and as Attorney General, and in 1821 was elected to the United States Senate. He was a man of sincere causes, whether fighting to abolish the law that imprisoned a man for his debts or opposing the extension of the slave trade. He resigned from a second term in the Senate to become Governor of New York, but two months later he had returned to the national capital as Jackson's Secretary of State.

So Van Buren, dazzling drab Washington with his peacock colors, was a man of demonstrated abilities—self-confident, cheerful, and quite unprepared for the disaster awaiting him. He had been President for two months when the Panic of 1837 struck like a thunderclap. On May 10th banks in New York City closed. On May 12th banks in Philadelphia shut down. Soon no bank in the country could meet the demands for payments in gold and silver and the panic became a fear carried on the wind.

"Closed" signs appeared like smallpox warnings on stores, offices and factories. Farmers found diminishing markets for their produce. The unemployed roamed the streets—bewildered, resentful, and growing angrier as the grim, hungry weeks piled up. A skimpy wheat crop raised the price of flour and the poor rioted in the streets of New York City, crying for bread. Plantation owners could not sell their cotton. As imports dropped off, empty ships moaned in the tides beside deserted wharves.

Van Buren, driving around Washington in a beautiful olive-green coach with silver-mounted harness and liveried footmen, endeared himself to few. Nor did his daughter-in-law, who acted as mistress of the White House, arouse kind comment for the courtly manner with which she received guests while wearing a gaudy dress with three ostrich plumes, seated in an armchair on a raised platform. Van Buren's solution to the money shortages of the panic was to establish an independent national treasury—not a new idea, but one that he finally forced on Congress.

In the midst of these troubles Van Buren's administration was brought to the brink of armed conflict with Great Britain by a curious little affair sometimes called the Aroostook War. At the root of this disorder in 1837 were revolts in the provinces of Upper and Lower Canada to secure a greater degree of self-government. The leader of the Upper Canadian rebels was William Lyon Mackenzie, whose force of about six hundred raiders fled to a base on an island in the Niagara River.

American sympathy strongly favored Mackenzie's rebels. With good reason he believed that the supplies he so badly needed could be brought from Buffalo, where the steamboat *Caroline* stood loaded at the dock. British troops, alert to this scheme, invaded American soil, burned the *Caroline*, and killed an American citizen.

The northern border seethed with threats of revenge. Many Americans joined with Mackenzie or aided him financially. Soon the Thousand Islands became the hideout of rebels bent on revenge. The *Sir Robert Peel*, a Canadian vessel, was destroyed. Wisely Van Buren sent General Scott to these scenes of trouble. With firmness and tact the President settled the affair, but such was the bitter feeling toward Van Buren that he received scant credit for even his successes.

Yet despite financial disaster and the war scare on the northern border, the America of Van Buren's one unhappy term in the Presidency could count many gains. Charles Goodyear discovered his vulcanizing process in 1839, and the following year the first regular transatlantic steamship service was inaugurated and the magnetic telegraph patented. Van Buren died on July 24, 1862 in Kinderhook, the city of his birth.

60

WILLIAM HENRY HARRISON

"Tippecanoe and Tyler, Too!"

LIKE a noiseless shadow, the scout slipped from behind the tree. "Shawnees!" he hissed. "At least three hundred murdering Shawnees coming straight for Vincennes behind that peacock, Tecumseh!"

At a full gallop the scout rode his pony into Vincennes. One thing he could say for the government in Washington. When they picked a tough Indian fighter like William Henry Harrison to run the northwest territory, they chose the right man.

William Henry Harrison first decided to go West when, as a young medical student at Hampden Sidney College, he read reports of Indian outrages along the western frontier. An obstinate guardian objected to a military career for the son of one of Virginia's distinguished signers of the Declaration of Independence, but another old friend of the Harrison family, George Washington, interceded in William's behalf.

As a young soldier under the old Revolutionary War hero, Mad

Anthony Wayne, William Henry Harrison quickly justified Washington's faith in him. His courage in battle was matched by a calm judgment in dealing with people. Wise old-timers smiled when they watched Harrison. This young fellow would make his mark. When part of the northwest territory was organized into the new territory of Indiana, that prediction came true, for Harrison was appointed Governor of an area that included the present states of Indiana, Illinois, Michigan and Wisconsin.

Presidents Jefferson and Madison both continued Harrison in the Governor's office, and the words that described him as an administrator were "capable," "patient," "just," "fearless." He ignored hostile speculators and divided the public lands into small tracts for the welfare of poor settlers. He organized the legislature that now convened at Vincennes. With the best interest of the Indians at heart, he tried to prevent the sale of intoxicating liquors among them, and to introduce inoculations for smallpox. Through a treaty with several tribes, in 1809 he purchased for the nation about 3,000,000 acres of land along the Wabash and White rivers. Common sense, hard work, quiet determination, and steady trigger-finger—every quality that Harrison possessed frontiersmen admired.

But Harrison had a powerful enemy in Tecumseh. Greedy, unfair, the Indian's foe—in such terms the chief described the palefaced Governor. And the Shawnees listened.

Harrison wanted peace. He knew that the Shawnees were hungry, so he gave them provisions from the public stores since any man, white or red, became more reasonable on a full stomach. And it was at Harrison's invitation that on a bright August day in 1810 Tecumseh and the Shawnees came to Vincennes. The conference started poorly. Invited to the Governor's house, Tecumseh answered haughtily:

"Houses were built for you to hold councils in. Indians hold theirs in the open air."

Harrison tried to conciliate Tecumseh by inviting him to sit near his "father" and again the chief's retort amounted to an insult:

"The sun is my father, and the earth is my mother, and on her bosom I will repose."

Tecumseh had no ear for any proposition except the return of the lands along the Wabash and White rivers. The dreams for America of the white man and red were as far apart as their customs. The following year, when a number of Indian raids brought death to the frontier, Harrison endeavored to reason once more with the chief who claimed the sun for his father. Tecumseh professed friendship, then journeyed among the Creeks, Choctaws and Cherokees, organizing them against the settlers.

By now Harrison had his fill of Tecumseh. Joy swept the territory with the news that Harrison was calling for volunteers.

"Boys, you know that Indian town on the upper Wabash—the place called Tippecanoe?" settlers shouted. "Harrison's going to build a fort there. He'll stop those raids!"

By the hundreds, volunteers poured into Vincennes.

On a raw November day in 1811 Harrison marched his ragtag frontier army almost to Tippecanoe. The Indians asked for a parley. "All right," Harrison replied, but he expected trickery.

Before dawn the Indians struck. Shrill war whoops rose on every side. Guns flashed in the darkness. Knives slashed.

"Boys, keep your aim low," Harrison growled.

Daylight, filtering through the forest, brought a sparkle to Harrison's eyes. Now he could use his cavalry!

"Ride 'em down!" ran the shout.

There was a cavalry charge—frontier style—with sabres, hunting knives and clubs. The kind of weapon didn't matter as long as it would topple an Indian. And topple Indians Harrison's charge did that morning at Tippecanoe. It toppled them so well that President Madison praised Harrison in a message to Congress and the legislatures of Kentucky and Indiana voted special thanks to the General.

But Harrison was not finished with Tecumseh. The War of 1812

gave the wily Shawnee chief a powerful ally in the British, and, informed by them that a comet would soon appear, he told the Creeks that they should fight the whites when they saw his arm stretching across the sky like a pale fire. A Creek chief objected and Tecumseh answered angrily:

"You do not believe that the Great Spirit has sent me. You shall believe it. I will go straight to Detroit, and when I get there I will stamp my foot upon the ground and shake down every house in Toockabatcha!"

In December, 1813, an earthquake unexpectedly occurred. Creeks ran from their houses, shouting: "Tecumseh is at Detroit!"

Marching steadily upon the British and their Creek allies was an American army under Harrison. The great battle of Thames resulted. Again a cavalry charge shattered the enemy and Tecumseh was killed. Once more Harrison became a national hero.

Terms in Congress and the Senate and an ambassadorship in South America followed for Harrison. Although once defeated for the Presidency, the Whigs decided to run him in 1840 with John Tyler of Virginia as his running mate.

Harrison's opponent was aristocratic, fancily dressed Martin Van Buren, and Harrison gained tremendous popularity with the people as the plain, unaffected "Log Cabin and Hard Cider" candidate. The catchy campaign slogan of "Tippecanoe and Tyler, too!" swept the country. Whereas Harrison won over Van Buren by only 146,900 popular votes, he achieved a smashing electoral majority of 234 votes to 60.

As ninth President, Harrison instantly became a Washington curiosity. In his sixty-eighth year the old Indian fighter still believed that he possessed boundless stamina. Without warning he appeared in government offices, looking for inefficient Federal employees to fire. Early each morning he left the White House to do his own marketing. Chill winds that March should have warned him to wear an overcoat.

A cold developed into pneumonia and within thirty days after taking office, the President was dead.

JOHN TYLER

"Honest John"

THE SOBER blue eyes of the tall, thin man took careful aim.
"Miss, Papa!" the children shrieked. "Don't win all the time!"

The marble went straight to its mark. Straightening up, the man
chuckled, then noticed the rider galloping through Williamsburg. The
horseman pulled rein, introduced himself as the chief clerk from the office
of the Secretary of State, and handed the marble player an envelope.

John Tyler, who had known nothing of the President's illness, thus
learned of Harrison's death. Called "Turncoat Tyler" by his enemies and
"Honest John" by his friends, the tall, thin man prepared at once for the
long journey to become the tenth President of the United States.

The memories of fifty-one years filled that journey for John Tyler.
All through his life there had been a point beyond which he would give
no quarter, as even the tyrant who had been his early schoolmaster discovered. That ill-tempered individual, William McMurdo, enjoyed using
a birch switch so vigorously that Tyler declared:

"It was a wonder he did not whip all the sense out of his scholars."

At the age of eleven Tyler became one of the ringleaders of the rebellion against McMurdo. By sheer force of numbers the boys overpowered their tormentor, tied his hands and feet and locked him in the schoolhouse. A passing traveler heard McMurdo's cries and released him.

By the age of seventeen, when Tyler graduated from William and Mary, he had learned to depend less on brawn and more on his quick mind to win an argument. Within two years he had been permitted to practice law and in another two years had been elected to the Virginia Legislature. Since then he had held various positions of public trust—as a member of Congress and the Senate, as a judge, as Governor of Virginia, and for one short month as Vice-President of the United States—and one trait he shared with John Quincy Adams. Never did any two men more earnestly put the dictates of conscience ahead of party affiliation.

For Tyler, a principle was not always a question of telling black from white. In the bitter debates that produced the Missouri Compromise, he admitted frankly that he was against continuing the institution of slavery, and yet he opposed any restriction on the extension of slavery. These apparently conflicting views Tyler explained by asserting that the wider the area over which slavery was spread, the quicker it would disappear! In the nullification crisis it became difficult for him to decide which he disliked more—the high-handed action taken by South Carolina or President Jackson's preparations to use force. Yet he spoke out sharply against the "gag-rule" as denying the constitutional guarantee of the right of petition.

The Whig Party that nominated Harrison for President had selected Tyler as its vice-presidential candidate for the sole purpose of attracting other "turncoat Democrats" to the ticket. Obviously no Whig in his right mind had expected Harrison to die, thus saddling the party with a Democrat as its leader. But here was John Tyler on his way to Washington.

The ambition of Henry Clay already had nettled Harrison, who

The Gazette

TEXAS ANNEXED

Stanley Dersh

had told the Kentuckian rather coldly: "You seem to forget, sir, that it is I who am President!" Clay, who fancied himself the white hope of the Whigs, certainly had less patience with an "accident" of a President like Tyler. The old issue of the national bank, which Clay supported and Tyler opposed as unconstitutional, became the double-edged sword with which the two men dueled, virtually to the point of political death. Clay controlled Congress and forced through his bill on the bank. Tyler vetoed it. An outraged Clay forced through a similar bill. Tyler vetoed that also.

Washington was torn apart by the rancorous feud. Plots to assassinate Tyler were openly discussed. With the exception of Daniel Webster every member of Tyler's Cabinet resigned. One night an angry mob, armed with clubs, and inflamed with whisky, marched on the White House. Overrunning the lawn of the presidential mansion, they shouted insults at Tyler, hurled stones and broke windows, but Tyler had armed the members of his staff and there the damage ended. For the first time in history a resolution was introduced in the Senate to impeach the President, but Democrats united with Whigs to defeat the measure.

The other great issue that dominated "Honest John's" unhappy years in the Presidency was the dispute over the annexation of Texas, which had won its independence from Mexico in 1836. Like most Southerners, Tyler favored annexation, and concluded a treaty with the Republic of Texas for that purpose. The President could count on his enemies by now, and in the Senate they followed their habitual behavior by refusing to ratify the treaty. A strong statement in favor of annexation by James K. Polk, the Democratic nominee for President, finally saved the treaty and Tyler was able to sign it on March 3, 1845—his last day in office!

A second marriage in Tyler's final year as President added another "first" to his record as the first Chief Executive to be wed in the White House, and for once he aroused public interest without a threatened shower of brickbats. He left with his new bride to live at Sherwood Forest, his estate on the James River, where he died on January 18, 1862.

JAMES KNOX POLK

"Napoleon of the Stump"

COARSE, angry and stubborn, delegates to the 1844 Democratic Convention in Baltimore refused after seven ballots to give a two-thirds majority to either Martin Van Buren or to the favorite of the western men, Lewis Cass of Michigan, as their presidential nominee. So onto the American political scene stepped the first "dark horse"—a man nobody had expected to be President, and who was acceptable as a candidate since he soothed angry emotions and offered a way out of the deadlock. His name was James Knox Polk, and on the ninth ballot he won the nomination.

The Whigs asked derisively, "Who's Polk?" To their own sorrow, they learned the answer. The vital issue before the nation in 1844 was the annexation of Texas. Henry Clay, the Whig candidate for President, hedged on the question in an effort to satisfy both anti-slavery and pro-slavery opinion. Polk's stand, in contrast, was firm and clear. He shared the feeling of John Quincy Adams and Andrew Jackson that Texas should not have been ceded to Spain in 1819. The territory, he argued, should be annexed as a valuable part of the Mississippi Valley and sound military judgment supported his position that as long as any foreign power controlled the upper waters of the Red River, the security of New Orleans was endangered. The Whigs continued to shout sarcastically, "Who's Polk?" until the vote of the electoral college was announced—175 for Polk, 105 for Clay. Then they knew who Polk was—the eleventh President of the United States.

Although Polk served only one term in the Presidency and never lived down his unpopularity with Northerners opposed to slavery, he was actually one of the most successful men ever to occupy the White House. His life began on November 2, 1795 in a humble log cabin in Mecklenburg County, North Carolina, but soon his family moved across the mountains to the beautiful, fertile country along Tennessee's Duck River and here young Polk spent a happy boyhood helping his father as a farmer and surveyor. The lad's alert mind was apparent to his teachers and private tutors, and they were not surprised when, in 1818, he was graduated from the University of North Carolina with special honors in the classics and in mathematics.

Old Felix Grundy, the best lawyer in Tennessee, accepted Polk as a student and within a year the youth passed his bar examination. Polk's instant success as a lawyer resulted from his exceptional ability as an orator and admiring friends called him the "Napoleon of the Stump." In politics the same gift contributed to his rapid rise, and he was successively elected to the Tennessee House of Representatives, to the United States Congress, and Governor of Tennessee.

A short man, never very robust, honest and industrious but often as cold in manner as a codfish, Polk's strength was his intense party loyalty. In his view, only Democrats deserved to enter heaven. During Jackson's stormy eight years in the White House, Polk supported the President so

BUENA VISTA

Stanley Borsch

steadfastly that he was nicknamed "Young Hickory." He served under Van Buren with the same unwavering devotion to the party.

Polk reached Washington as President knowing precisely what he intended to accomplish. His first message to Congress revealed that he meant to deal firmly with Mexico on the question of Texas. Already he had dispatched the American Army under General Zachary Taylor to occupy the western bank of the Nueces River, where it faced country over which Texas never had exercised recognized jurisdiction. On December 29, 1844 Texas was admitted to the Union, and then, at the suggestion of General Taylor, American forces advanced toward the Rio Grande. Now in thoroughly disputed country, as far as any American claim could be made, Taylor came face to face with Mexican troops. Battles at Palo Alto and Resaca de la Palma drove the Mexicans across the Rio Grande, and charging that American blood had been shed on American soil, Polk asked Congress to declare war on Mexico.

An ungainly young fellow from Illinois, serving for the first time in Congress, joined the Whig outcry that Polk had "unnecessarily and un-constitutionally" started a war. And it was this same young congressman —his name was Abraham Lincoln—who introduced into the House the famous "spot resolutions" demanding that the President indicate the exact spot where American blood had been shed.

"Let him answer with *facts*, and not with arguments," Lincoln orated scornfully. "Let him remember he sits where Washington sat, and so remembering let him answer, as Washington would answer."

Lincoln was having a wonderful time in his first fling in national politics, and by his view, if one accepted his statements too literally, only Whigs deserved to enter heaven. Perhaps one reason why Polk never has been remembered too kindly in history has stemmed from the attacks against him by Lincoln, who was destined to outshine every President except Washington.

Yet it was a northern member of Polk's own party, David Wilmot of

Pennsylvania, who truly stigmatized the President as a willing puppet for slavery advocates. In large degree, the organized agitation between anti-slavery and pro-slavery forces that led eventually to a civil war began with the proposal that became known as the "Wilmot Proviso." In any territory acquired through the Mexican War, this legislation insisted, "neither slavery nor involuntary slavery shall ever exist...except for crime, whereof the party shall first be duly convicted."

The "Wilmot Proviso" acted like a magnet in drawing together Whigs and Northern Democrats opposed to the extension of slavery. Lincoln recalled that he voted for it "more than forty times," disclosing how doggedly it was used as a political weapon against the pro-slavery interests. The "Wilmot Proviso" would pop up as an amendment to bills for money to carry on the War with Mexico and even as an amendment to legislation for settling the boundary of the Oregon border. The Democrats killed the "Wilmot Proviso" in the Senate, but political scars had been inflicted that never really healed. Meanwhile, the War in Mexico ended and the country extended its southwestern boundary to the Rio Grande and added to the national domain the provinces of New Mexico and Upper California.

As a War President, Polk, indeed, had been a man of success! He

was equally fortunate with his tariff policies, and no fair-minded person really could argue with the principle on which he insisted: "The farmer, or planter, who toils yearly in his fields, is engaged in 'domestic industry,' and is as much entitled to have his labor 'protected' as the manufacturer, the man of commerce, the navigator, or the mechanic, who are engaged also in 'domestic industry' in their different pursuits." With like skill he reached a settlement with Great Britain of our boundary in the northwest — it was fixed at the 49th parallel of north latitude.

Life in America changed in other ways during Polk's four years in the Presidency. Wisconsin and Iowa joined with Texas as new states in the Union. Gold was discovered in California, the United States Naval Academy was established at Annapolis, and people began pasting postage stamps on their letters. The invention of the rotary printing press heralded an age when newspapers and magazines would be more widely distributed, and the patenting of the sewing machine promised to reduce the work in American households.

Many old patterns of behavior were crumbling, even in the White House where the President's wife, a woman of deep religious convictions, abolished the custom of serving refreshments and forbade dancing. Yet Mrs. Polk was an extremely popular hostess and a woman of great personal charm, sincerity and beauty. President Polk was admired by his friends for his good mind and industrious habits, but the slavery question had aroused violent passions and his enemies were numerous and scornful. Their growing bitterness, based on the belief that the Mexican War had been a reckless adventure to expand the domain of the slaveholders, blinded them to the President's achievements.

In accepting the nomination at Baltimore in 1844, Polk had stipulated that he would serve for only one term and he refused the renomination that he could easily have received. His health had felt the strain of official duty and shortly after he returned to his home in Nashville he fell ill. Within a few hours death came to him on June 15, 1849.

76

ZACHARY TAYLOR
"Old Rough and Ready"

THE OLD GENERAL and the young captain were warm friends, and neither guessed that one day they would both hold office as President of the United States. Sam Grant was receiving his first experience with war in Mexico and was proving even then that he was a capable, resourceful soldier. The young captain's idol was General Zachary Taylor, and in later years when Grant himself commanded vast armies there could be no question that he copied the style and methods he learned from "Old Rough and Ready."

Between Taylor and Winfield Scott, the other general under whom Grant served in Mexico, the contrasts were pronounced. Physically Scott was something of a buttertub who covered himself with all the showy uniform he could pull on, whereas the lean Taylor dressed sloppily and for comfort. Taylor, who sometimes fumbled for words in conversation, could write battle orders so clearly, a schoolboy could understand them.

"Both were pleasant to serve under—Taylor was pleasant to serve with," Sam Grant recalled. "Scott saw more through the eyes of his staff officers than through his own. His plans were deliberately prepared, and fully expressed in orders. Taylor saw for himself, and gave orders to meet the emergency without reference to how they would read in history."

Soldiering was almost the only life Zachary Taylor knew from cradle to grave. Born on November 24, 1784 in Orange County, Virginia, he was the son of Colonel Richard Taylor, a hero of the Revolutionary War. A year later the family moved to Kentucky, where liberal grants of land were given to soldiers, and here Zachary grew up among neighbors who never tired of discussing the battles in which they had fought. In the sparsely settled farming country Kentucky was then, opportunities for formal schooling were few, but Zachary never lacked for lessons in how to handle troops, mass artillery, march an army or flush out an enemy with a bayonet charge.

Taylor's first military experience came during the troubles along the frontier when Tecumseh was at the peak of his power. In June, 1812, the valley of the Wabash trembled with the fear of an Indian invasion, and Taylor marched his little band, about fifty strong, to protect Vincennes. The savages appeared in large numbers, expecting to capture this river stockade with ease. But Taylor had been raised on the tales of too many old soldiers to be outwitted. Skillfully he met attack with attack and ruse with ruse. By October, when the remainder of the army arrived, there wasn't a hostile Indian in the valley.

In succeeding years Taylor rose both in rank and renown as an Indian fighter. He commanded at Fort Snelling, then the advance post in the northwest, and later at Fort Crawford near Prairie du Chien. In 1836 he was sent to Florida to put down the Seminole uprising and smashed that rebellion at the decisive battle of Okeechobee. Soon he was honored with the rank of a general and four years later given command of the southern division of the western army.

When war threatened with Mexico over the annexation of Texas, Taylor's advance from the Nueces River toward Fort Brown on the Rio Grande produced the first great battle. Taylor moved boldly with 2,288 men against whom the Mexican general, Arista, could throw a force of at least 6,000. Taylor's subordinate officers called for a council of war and urged him to fall back, awaiting re-enforcements.

"I shall go to Fort Brown or stay in my shoes," retorted Taylor, using the western expression for "to do or die."

At dawn Taylor attacked. The chaparral—dense copses of thorn-bushes—shielded the enemy and impeded the action of the Americans. Taylor pressed on that day and the next. Mexican batteries pounded his advance and he saw his dragoons charge forward gallantly, snatching the blazing cannon from the hands of Arista's gunners. When the Mexicans began counting their losses—1,000 dead against 49 American casualties —they knew how badly they had been beaten. Taylor marched on to Fort Brown where he could take off his shoes—in comfort.

The country thrilled to the stories of Taylor's victories in Mexico. "Old Rough and Ready" winning on the Rio Grande—or sweeping the field at Monterey—or at Buena Vista, cutting to pieces the army of Santa

Anna, the hated villain of the massacre in the Alamo—so mounted the triumphs that made Taylor a national hero.

What the general knew about politics could be hidden in a thimble, and his only ambition after the war was to take up the life of a farmer. Drafted by the Whigs as a presidential candidate, Taylor was helped by a split among the Democrats, who ran Lewis Cass as the regular nominee and Van Buren as the candidate of a splinter group, the Free-soilers. Taylor won a plurality of the popular vote and 163 of 290 votes in the electoral college.

"Well," commented General Scott, "Taylor is an upright man."

"No," replied Mrs. Scott, "he is a downright man."

Both were correct, for Taylor was upright in principle and downright honest. Perhaps, as tradition insisted, his wife smoked a corncob pipe in the privacy of her room in the White House. Anyone who saw the President in his baggy clothes, a high hat pushed on the back of his head, understood that the Taylors hadn't come to Washington to put on airs. Taylor appointed his Cabinet on the advice of others for, in a political sense, he had neither friends to reward nor enemies to punish.

In Congress sounded the growlish rumble of the growing storm over slavery produced by the settlements that must be made over the status of the territory acquired from Mexico. Taylor stood squarely for the Union, and would yield nothing to the South, and on this position he divided with his Vice-President, Millard Fillmore.

Taylor had held office as our twelfth President for sixteen months when exposure to the sun during a July Fourth celebration afflicted the old warrior with a high fever. Within five days he was dead. His son-in-law, Jefferson Davis, became President of the Confederacy and his son, Richard, served as a general in the Southern armies, but in the fast approaching war that often split the loyalties of families, there can be no assurance that "Old Rough and Ready" would have followed their course. He was, after all, an upright, downright man, who spoke and acted for himself.

80

MILLARD FILLMORE

"The Last Whig"

NOT EVERY PRESIDENT of the United States could claim among his forebears a great-grandfather who had been captured by pirates. For nearly nine months John Fillmore endured the cruel hardships of a slave sailing under the black flag before the chance came to smash an ax into the skull of the boatswain, seize the ship, and sail her back into Boston Harbor. This same strain of aggressive self-reliance was still running strong in the Fillmores when Millard was born on January 7, 1800. And the trait was one that all the Fillmores needed, for none of them ever seemed able to accumulate much earthly wealth so that life for them was always an unremitting struggle against the wolf at the door.

By the time Millard entered the world, the Fillmore family had moved from Massachusetts to the then bleak wilderness of New York's Finger Lakes country. The boy who one day would become our thirteenth President grew up in a drab log cabin where the only books were the Bible and a hymnal. Nine months of the year he toiled at helping his father grub a spare livelihood from a frontier farm, and the other three he attended a one-room schoolhouse. Here at least he learned to like Miss Abigail Powers, his teacher, for in later years he married this pretty redhead.

Meanwhile circumstances went from bad to worse for the Fillmores and at the age of fourteen Millard was apprenticed to a cloth-maker. The merchant was harsh in speech, rough in manner and unjust in treatment. One day when the man threatened to punish Millard, the boy raised an ax and told him to come ahead—at the risk of his life! Happily the tempers of both cooled, and Millard bought his freedom from the cloth-maker for thirty dollars. Wrapping his few clothes and some bread and dried venison in a knapsack, the lad walked home through more than a hundred miles of virgin forests.

"I think that this injustice—which was no more than other apprentices have suffered and will suffer—had a marked effect on my character," Fillmore said afterward. "It made me feel for the weak and unprotected, and to hate the insolent tyrant in every station of life."

As Millard Fillmore grew to manhood he became a handsome fellow, standing over six feet. Pretty Miss Powers helped him at the study of law and he began his practice in Aurora, New York, where he won his first case and pocketed the princely fee of four dollars. By conscientious study he advanced steadily as a barrister, and his eloquence in court drew him to the notice of the supporters of the young Whig Party. Fillmore's political career followed the up-and-down pattern that had characterized many activities of his family for six generations in America. He was three times elected to Congress, failed in a bid to become Governor of New York, and then was elected State Comptroller. As a loyal, lifelong Whig he was rewarded in 1848 with the vice-presidential nomination and rode into office on the coat-tails of Zachary Taylor.

Now that the Mexican War had ended, the country grappled with the explosive problem of slavery in the territory that had been acquired.

In the Senate the three great giants of American politics—Daniel Webster of Massachusetts, Henry Clay of Kentucky and John C. Calhoun of South Carolina—were locked in the scalding debates from which the Compromise of 1850 emerged. Unlike Taylor, Fillmore sided with the constitutional argument that slavery should be free to spread wherever it would, and with Taylor's death the South thus won a strong ally in Fillmore's elevation to the Presidency. The crux of the Compromise of 1850 was the admission of California as a free state in return for a severe Fugitive Slave Law, but Fillmore never guessed when he signed this measure that he was signing as well the death warrant of the Whig Party.

"What does the Fugitive Slave Law really mean?" cried indignant Northerners.

"It means," came the indignant answer, "that slaveowners, coming North, can claim any Negro they see as a runaway and though that Negro may have been free for years, they can carry him back to slavery!"

Inspired by the wave of horror over the Fugitive Slave Law, in 1852 Harriet Beecher Stowe published *Uncle Tom's Cabin*. This passionate novel wrung the hearts of people around the world and rivers of tears were wept for Uncle Tom, the mistreated, runaway slave.

Northerners who opposed slavery refused to think of Fillmore in any terms except that he had signed the abhorrent Fugitive Slave Law. In sending Commodore Perry on an expedition to Japan, trade was opened with that far-off empire—but Fillmore received no thanks for it. When, in 1851, the Library of Congress burned and the President and his Cabinet formed a bucket brigade and toiled long hours to extinguish the fire, Fillmore still failed to become a hero.

With dignity, the President stood his ground against his foes. He did what he thought right—including installing in the White House its first library, bathtub and cook stove. Jenny Lind, the "Swedish Nightingale" whose singing captivated America, was entertained by the Fillmores. The nation, reasonably, should have been in a more charitable

mood when, in June, 1851, in a race around the Isle of Wight, the yacht *America* defeated fourteen English yachts and brought home the "America's Cup."

But no event could divert many minds from the fact that Fillmore had signed the Fugitive Slave Law, and his popularity could not have suffered more if he had been caught beating Uncle Tom with his own hands. In 1856 he was nominated for President by the American or Know Nothing Party and experienced the humiliating defeat of carrying only the state of Maryland.

Thereafter until his death in Buffalo, New York on March 8, 1874, Fillmore lived a quiet, useful life. He owned the biggest mansion in the city, proof of how far he had come from the log cabin of his boyhood. Among the many important offices he filled was that of the first chancellor of the University of Buffalo. A sincere and modest man, during a trip to England he was invited by Oxford University to receive an honorary degree. Fillmore declined. He was unworthy of such an honor, he said.

FRANKLIN PIERCE

"Bleeding Kansas"

THE DARKEST "dark horse" ever elected President was Franklin Pierce. For thirty-five ballotings the Democratic Convention in 1852 tried unsuccessfully to settle on a candidate. Then the Virginia delegation proposed Pierce, hoping he could break the deadlock. Other delegations clung loyally to their favorite nominees, but on the forty-ninth ballot the tide to Pierce became a shattering wave as he rolled up 282 votes against 11 for his opponents. Again the country asked, as it had inquired when Polk had emerged as the first "dark horse":

"Well, who is he?"

Franklin Pierce had been a good general in the Mexican War, flung back the Democrats in an effort to match what little claim to glory the hopeless Whigs could make for their candidate, General Winfield Scott.

In New England the Democrats said:

"Ask anyone in New Hampshire what a fine lawyer and upstanding citizen Pierce is. Ask his old college mate and good friend, Nathaniel Hawthorne, what a keen mind he has. Look how well he handled himself when, in 1837, he was elected to the Senate as its youngest member."

And in the South the Democrats said:

"You can depend on Pierce. He was a solid supporter of the annexation of Texas and he told those Yankees to their faces that he would take both Texas and slavery, if necessary. He's for a Fugitive Slave Law as solid as Plymouth Rock. Pierce will tell you—the only thing wrong with this country is its loud-mouth abolitionists!"

By and large, every one of these statements was true. As a "dark horse" in the presidential race, Franklin Pierce possessed the ability to run forward, backward or sideways.

The tall, handsome man soon to become the nation's fourteenth President was born in Hillsborough, New Hampshire on November 23, 1804. His father, a distinguished officer in the Revolutionary War, was a farmer who quickly recognized Franklin's exceptional intelligence and sent him to good schools to prepare for Bowdoin College. Here Franklin's interest in military subjects almost led to his downfall since he devoted so much time to drilling a company of student-soldiers that at the end of his second year he stood at the bottom of his class. Scared stiff, he turned a new leaf and when he graduated in 1824, ranked third in his class.

Pierce's steady advancement, both in politics and in law, was a result of the expressive face, eloquent figure and clear, musical voice that combined to make him an excellent orator. He was courteous and kind, quick of mind and a diligent student of any subject that confronted him. His record in the Senate was creditable, and New England remembered especially that he had carried through a bill providing a pension for the aged widow of Isaac Davis, who had been among the first to fall during the Revolution in the battle at Concord Bridge.

In 1842 Pierce resigned from the Senate to devote his time to his family and law practice, and he was a man who obviously could stand by

a decision, for when President Polk offered him the appointment as United States Attorney General, he declined. Then the Mexican War revived the military interest that had almost cost him so dearly at Bowdoin, and Polk commissioned him a brigadier-general.

To claim that Pierce was as accomplished a general as Winfield Scott was political romancing, and yet Pierce, when he got a chance to fight in Mexico, came off a hero. In August of 1847 at the battle of Contreras, 7,000 Mexicans occupied a strongly intrenched camp. Scott's plan was to launch a frontal attack while another American force swept around the Mexican flank and cut off its retreat.

Pierce, leading the frontal assault, went in gamely. The flanking movement that was to support him bogged down, and there he stood—up to his neck in a battle across the crater of an extinct volcano where sharp, jagged rocks gave perfect cover to Mexican skirmishers. Pierce's horse stepped into a cleft between two rocks, breaking its leg and seriously injuring the General's knee. But Pierce pressed on, refusing the plea of a surgeon to retire from the field. Next morning he was still full of fight, keeping that Mexican front bristling with action, when Scott's flankers broke through on the enemy's rear and sent the Mexicans retreating in panic.

A man of quiet resolution, a two-fisted fighter, a thinker with strong Southern sympathies—for good reasons, the Democrats expected that their "dark horse" would run like the wind, and when the electoral vote was tallied Pierce had outdistanced his rival 254 to 42. Before leaving for Washington, the President saw one of his sons, a boy of eleven, killed before his eyes in a railroad wreck, and the nation grieved for the sad, heartbroken man who came to the White House. Yet personal tragedy could not soften the rough-and-tumble of politics. If Fillmore had reeled under the furor of the Fugitive Slave Law, his administration would seem easy and calm compared to the storm awaiting Pierce.

A bill introduced into the Senate to organize the territories of Kansas

and Nebraska permitted slavery north of the parallel of 36° 30', thus carrying slavery into a region where it had been prohibited since the days of the Missouri Compromise. The father of the Kansas-Nebraska Bill was Senator Stephen A. Douglas of Illinois, who obviously was playing for the Presidency by winning the support of Southern Democrats. Pierce backed the bill and it passed Congress in May, 1854. Slavery had won its greatest victory, but at a cost that was unexpected—a shooting war.

Rival legislatures were organized in Kansas. Armed bands from Missouri—the "Border Ruffians"—crossed into Kansas and with guns and terrorism helped the pro-slavery advocates form a government. Free-soilers cried, "Fraud!" The votes rolled up by the slavery convention were more than twice the number of settlers in the territory! The free-state forces then organized another government, framed a constitution that was adopted by a vote of 1,731 to 46, and elected Alfred H. Reeder their delegate to Congress.

Pierce had no sympathy for the Free-soilers in Kansas. He ignored the blunt fact that the majority of settlers in the territory favored admission to the Union as a free state. The Senate refused to recognize Reeder or his government. So "Bleeding Kansas" became a national tragedy as constant quarrels between pro-slavery and free-state factions brought bloodshed, the burning of buildings and looting. The terrible image of that half-crazed abolitionist, John Brown, haunted the Kansas countryside. In a raid on Potawatomie Creek old John Brown one night senselessly murdered five men.

Pierce's single term as President ended before the desperate struggle in "Bleeding Kansas" finally was won by the Free-soilers. As the railroads expanded toward the Pacific, farmers in the West and South grew prosperous and the Government's gold reserves piled up to the point where the tariff of 1857 reduced duties in order to cut down the Government's income. Through the Gadsden Purchase the United States secured from Mexico 45,535 square miles south of the Gila River, a region we now know as Arizona and New Mexico.

Yet none of these events during Pierce's administration held significance in the hearts of the American people beside the grim realization that the slavery question had erupted into a shooting war in Kansas. In the Democratic Convention of 1856 Pierce lacked the early support to win renomination and on the seventeenth ballot the presidential candidate became Senator James Buchanan of Pennsylvania. Pierce traveled in Europe until almost the outbreak of civil war. In an address to a Union mass meeting in Concord, New Hampshire, he urged the people to stand by the Federal Government. Until his death in Concord on October 8, 1869 he lived in quiet retirement among neighbors who respected him as a man of honest conviction and a warm heart.

JAMES BUCHANAN

"Old Buck"

WHEN JAMES BUCHANAN was inaugurated as the fifteenth President of the United States, he was almost sixty-six years of age. Except for William Henry Harrison, who had held office for only one month, he was then the oldest man to reside in the White House. "Old Buck" reached the Presidency because he hadn't made many enemies, yet when his term ended, he left fearing for his life.

As Minister to Great Britain, Buchanan had been out of the country at the time of the Kansas-Nebraska Bill, and the Democrats had nominated him as an affable "middle-of-the-roader" who should be acceptable to both North and South. In the electoral vote his victory seemed impressive—174 votes against 114 votes for John C. Fremont, the candidate for the new Republican Party, and 8 votes for Fillmore, the Know Nothing nominee. Although Buchanan carried every southern state except Maryland, he failed by 372,000 votes of winning a popular plurality, and the country knew that he owed his election to the "slavocrats."

A distinguished if somewhat frosty old gentleman, Buchanan had deserved his party's endorsement. Born April 23, 1791 on a farm near Mercersburg, Pennsylvania, he had worked hard to get ahead. He had done well as a student at Dickinson College and shown early promise as a capable lawyer and shrewd politician. At first a Federalist, he had opposed the War of 1812, but when the British threatened Baltimore, he had enlisted as a private in the army. Admiration for Andrew Jackson transformed Buchanan into a Democrat and he had served in Congress and the Senate and as Secretary of State in Polk's Cabinet.

"Old Buck's as worthy a President as we've ever elected," cried the Democrats, denying that Buchanan owed an apology to anyone for his victory. Nonetheless Buchanan reached the White House a marked man.

A harmless, good-humored Negro named Dred Scott was Buchanan's nemesis. Once owned as a slave in Missouri by an army surgeon, Dred was taken by his master into the free state of Illinois and then into that region of the Wisconsin Territory where slavery had been prohibited by the Missouri Compromise. When, in 1838, the army surgeon returned to Missouri, he left Dred behind, hiring him out and then selling him.

But could Dred remain a slave in free territory? In 1846 Dred sued for his freedom and one state court decided that he was free and another that he wasn't. So Dred's famous case went into the Federal courts and the nation's temper, ablaze over "Bleeding Kansas," awaited the outcome.

The United States Supreme Court rendered its decision two days after Buchanan's inauguration, and the country knew that the President had concurred in the surprising verdict. In deciding that the court actually had no jurisdiction over the case and that, therefore, Dred must remain a slave, the decision could have weathered criticism even though five justices of the court were Southerners and seven were Democrats. But the court deliberately exploded political dynamite in the further opinion that the Missouri Compromise had been unconstitutional and that slavery could not be excluded from any territory.

In legal language, for a court to decide on an issue not specifically involved in a case is called *obiter dicta*, and on this basis the young Republican Party took the Dred Scott decision to the people as evidence of how the "slavocrats," with the help of the Democrats, had stolen the Supreme Court along with everything else in the country. No matter in what direction Buchanan tried now to steer his ship of state, he foundered upon the rocks of angry dissension. In Kansas, the Free-staters gained control. In Illinois, Abraham Lincoln in his debates with Senator Douglas gained national fame by insisting that the country could not remain "a house divided"—it could not endure half-slave and half-free.

Then on the night of October 16, 1859, crazed old John Brown with about twenty followers struck at Harper's Ferry, Virginia. Brown holed up in the Federal arsenal, awaiting the uprising among the slaves that he believed his bold action would inspire. No revolt occurred and Brown and his little band were captured by troops under the command of Colonel Robert E. Lee. Convicted of treason, Brown was hanged on December second—to the South a scoundrel who deserved to die on the gallows, but to many Northerners a martyr who had given his life in the cause of freedom. Like *Uncle Tom's Cabin* and Dred Scott, John Brown became a powerful, if indirect cause of civil war. Borrowing the melody of a

Southern hymn, soon Northerners would taunt the South by singing:
John Brown's body lies a-mouldering in his grave,
His soul goes marching on.

In the rising crisis Buchanan was pictured in the North as a flustered, weak, silly old man who was selling out the country to the "slavocrats." Were not the most influential men in his Cabinet, his enemies asked, avowed secessionists like Howell Cobb of Georgia, John Floyd of Virginia and Jacob Thompson of Mississippi? Was not one of his closest friends and most trusted advisors Mississippi's Jefferson Davis? Poor Buchanan almost needed friends and advisors wherever he could find them, for his own party was falling apart between Northern and Southern factions.

A gold strike in Colorado, the establishment of the Pony Express, the laying of the Atlantic cable, the admission of the new states of Minnesota, Oregon and Kansas—for these positive events during Buchanan's term in office the country had no absorbing interest. The prospect of a Republican victory in 1860, shattering the alliance by which the South had held influence over occupants of the White House since Fillmore's administration, filled the air with a dread of approaching civil war.

With Lincoln's election, South Carolina seceded and in the glum weeks that followed six other states joined her in forming the Confederate States of America. Buchanan seemed helpless to stop the break-up of the Union. Too late, when Federal forces under Major Robert Anderson occupied Fort Sumter in Charleston Harbor, the President appeared to stand firmly against the hotheads in his own party. But by then the damage had been done.

A sad, weary old man of almost seventy years, Buchanan made the long journey from Washington to his home in Lancaster, Pennsylvania. In later years he published a vigorous defense of his policies as President, but the nation remembered his years in the White House as belonging to other men—Dred Scott, John Brown and Abraham Lincoln. When civil war came, Buchanan supported the Union. He died June 1, 1868.

Stanley Dersh

ABRAHAM LINCOLN

"Honest Abe"

ALONG THE planked sidewalks of Chicago's muddy streets a thousand jaunty marchers followed a brightly uniformed band.

"Yippee for Seward!" they shouted. "Hurray for William H. Seward, next President of the United States!"

Behind thumping drums happy supporters of Seward poured into the huge wooden Wigwam that Chicago had built for its first national political convention.

"Those New Yorkers are sure whooping it up," onlookers observed with a grin. "The Republican candidate will be Seward. Nobody can beat him!"

But others weren't so sure. "How about Lincoln?" they asked.

"*Lincoln!*" snorted the Seward men. "That prairie politician! He hasn't got a chance!"

"Honest Abe's popular with the people," the others retorted. "He talks common sense."

"Now lookit," said the Seward men, huffed at such ridiculous opposition, "Seward's been a governor and a distinguished senator. He's been to England and has dined with the Queen. Where do you think your Illinois Rail Splitter would get in London? Royal woodchoppers come cheap!"

The Lincoln men smiled in a way that said: "Ah, but this is Chicago —not London or Washington or New York!" They waited quietly while Seward's name was put in nomination. A reporter for a Cincinnati newspaper described the scene that followed:

"Hundreds of persons stopped their ears in pain. The shouting was absolutely frantic, shrill and wild. No Comanches, no panthers ever struck a higher note, or gave screams with more infernal intensity." Looking down from the stage, the reporter saw "a black, mighty swarm of hats" that were "flying with the velocity of hornets over a mass of human heads, most of the mouths of which were open."

But now came Lincoln's turn in this battle of lungs. Imagine all the hogs ever slaughtered in Cincinnati giving their death squeals in unison, said the reporter, and that's how the Lincoln boys outblasted their rivals. Moreover, they accompanied their yells "with stamping that made every plank and pillar in the building quiver."

With a total of 233 votes necessary to win the nomination, the tally at the end of the first ballot stood 173½ for Seward, 102 for Lincoln, and 198½ votes divided among ten other candidates. The Wigwam bordered on hysteria as the second balloting began. New Hampshire gave Lincoln a slight gain. Vermont came to him in a solid block. The building almost burst apart when Pennsylvania switched forty-four votes to "Honest Abe," bringing the new total to 184½ for Seward and 181 for Lincoln.

On the third ballot the trend to the Rail Splitter grew stronger. Men scribbled down each state's vote until Lincoln stood a vote and a half short of victory. The chairman of the Ohio delegation gained recognition.

"O-hi-o," he yelled, "changes four votes to A-bra-ham Lin-coln!"

The shout of joy that followed just missed ripping the roof off the Wigwam. Through the streets of Chicago ran the cry:

"Fire the salute! Abe Lincoln is nominated!"

And over the wires to Springfield, Illinois, home of the lucky candidate, sped a telegram: "We did it glory to God."

No one can be sure what thoughts passed through the mind of the tall, spare man as he read that telegram. But one day, after he had been elected President, he told a regiment of Ohio soldiers:

"I happen temporarily to occupy this big White House. I am a living witness that any of your children may look to come here as my father's child has."

It would have caused a laugh the length of Hardin County, Kentucky, if Tom Lincoln had told Nancy that February 12, 1809 when their baby boy arrived, "Some day Abe'll be President." Nancy would have smiled, for she was a gentle, good-humored woman, knowing a joke when she heard one. Her Tom was a practical dirt farmer, and that's what Abe would grow up to be.

Poor Nancy never really had a chance to understand how different Abe was for she died of a strange frontier illness called the "milk-sick" when the lad was ten. Her gentleness was in him—that she knew. Once he shot a wild turkey, then put the gun away forever. Killing went hard against his nature. And from his Pa he took the streak of rugged honesty, a willingness to work hard, and maybe that dislike for slavery which, many folk declared, led Tom Lincoln to move across the Ohio River into southwestern Indiana.

Young Abraham was eight years old then, and what he remembered most about his new wilderness home were the "many bears and other wild animals still in the woods." After his mother died his sister, eleven-year-old Sarah, tried to care for the family, but that was a rough time for all and Tom Lincoln saw at last the only right thing for him to do was to

marry again. Say what you will about Tom Lincoln—he picked good women. Sarah Bush Johnston, the widow he brought to the backwoods cabin, was sweet and gentle like Nancy. Abe fell in love with her.

Like Nancy, Stepmother Sarah insisted that Abe get what learning he could from the poor lot of traveling schoolmasters who came into the wilderness. Once Abe reckoned up all the formal schooling he had received and doubted if it amounted to a year. Yet he learned to read and write in that time, and to figure sums. He was a tall boy, hard as the fence rails he could split, a worker who could always "hire out" to a neighbor. He clerked in a store for a time, and ferried passengers from a boat landing on the Ohio to passing steamers fifteen miles away, and once with a neighbor's son floated a flatboat loaded with produce to New Orleans.

So he learned by seeing, and by reading a few books by firelight, and by being around people. Sometimes he was seized with a hankering to tell a story, or to speak the serious side of his mind. He'd climb up on a stump and the people would gather round. He could make them laugh —and listen—and keep coming back. They had never met anyone quite like him.

After fourteen years in Indiana, Tom Lincoln's fortunes hadn't gained by a hill of beans. Relatives in Illinois wrote of treeless prairies with deep black soil as fertile as a Garden of Eden. Then there was another epidemic of the "milk-sick," but Tom wasn't waiting to bury his wife this time. Abe, now twenty-one, drove one of the ox teams in the ten-day trek to the unbroken prairies along the Sangamon River. About ten miles west of the new town of Decatur, he helped his father put in the first crop.

The spring of 1831 got into Abe in a strange way, making him feel that he should strike off on his own. He remembered the settlement of New Salem he had seen on a bluff of the Sangamon. What led him to this straggling settlement of log cabins may have been a hunch that a nobody shouldn't start too fancy.

He arrived in New Salem—lanky, lumbering, likable, at loose ends. He helped run a store, and failed. He ran for the State Legislature, and lost. He studied surveying, became postmaster (since no one else seemed to want the job), and finally decided to try becoming a lawyer. From borrowed books he taught himself law. Next time he ran for the Legislature, he won.

Lots of stories were told about Abe after he was famous that no one could prove. Did he walk two miles to deliver a half pound of tea he had forgotten to give a customer? Well, maybe—he was that doggedly honest. Did he fall in love with pretty Ann Rutledge and grieve for the remainder of his life after she died? Again, just maybe—he was that devoted to the people he liked. Did he wrestle the town bully and stretch him flat on the grass? That story was true, for he possessed the strength of an ox.

What helped Lincoln get ahead—in New Salem, and after he moved to Springfield and hung out his shingle as a lawyer—was the fact that all sorts of people could trust him as a warm-hearted friend. He wasn't a lawyer who hunted up cases. He helped people, as best he could, looking on the human side of their legal troubles and talking sense with a smile that lighted up his face and made others forget what an ugly piece of physiognomy this fellow possessed. Combine with his innate affability a natural gift of gab, a keen mind, an ability to say a thing so anybody could understand what he meant, and the result was as natural as prairie mud after a rain—he succeeded at law, as a state legislator, and finally he was bound for Washington, as an earnest young congressman.

Lincoln served in Congress only two years, condemning the Mexican War as needless stupidity and supporting the Wilmot Proviso so that the slaveowners would gain precious little from the conflict, and then, as far as his political future was concerned, he dropped back on Springfield like a lump of lead. He sank so far out of sight, politically, that he seemed gone for good, and then the Kansas-Nebraska Bill and the Dred Scott decision brought him back with a rush.

"Slave states are places for poor white people to remove *from*, not to remove *to*," declared Lincoln, revealing that he could never forget the struggle of those Kentucky and Indiana years. The nation could not endure half-slave and half-free, but must become all one or the other, he said in his famous "House Divided" speech. And in his debates with Stephen A. Douglas for a seat in the Senate, Lincoln said that the struggle over slavery was as old as man's struggle between right and wrong or between freedom and tyranny—it was a struggle essentially against all who would say: "You work and toil and earn bread, and I'll eat it."

Lincoln lost the Senate race to Douglas, but he gained in national reputation and reduced the complex political quarrels of slavery to terms that people could understand. Meanwhile Douglas had said that he didn't care if slavery were voted up or down—it was up to settlers in the territories to decide their own status—which made him an unacceptable presidential candidate in the South. So the Democratic Party split in two, assuring Lincoln of victory at the polls.

What, actually, had happened in America was that as a single republic we had developed competing forms of democracy. In the agricultural South the old Greek model of democracy, based on slavery, had been followed. In the industrial North free labor had become essential to prosperity. Both parties to the national quarrel were honestly convinced, in their hearts, that they were right. A man who grits his teeth and clenches his fist and slams his hat on the floor tends to see himself as little David ready to slay Goliath. As a hero to his own emotions, he loses faith in written law and respect for judicial decisions. He grabs his sling-shot and dashes off to combat.

And that is what happened to the country in 1861. Lincoln came to the Presidency with his house truly divided now between the Union and the Confederate States of America. Through four bloody years of civil war, the struggle continued and changed until, at the end, the Emancipation Proclamation and the Thirteenth Amendment had given freedom to the slaves. Battles that staggered the imagination — Shiloh, Chancellorsville, Vicksburg, Gettysburg, among others—were written in blood-red letters into history. And new heroes arose—Robert E. Lee, who whipped a dozen Union generals before he came to grips with the plodding, equally brilliant Ulysses S. Grant, the joyous Jeb Stuart and little Phil Sheridan in his plumed hat, the jaunty Beauregard and the red-bearded William Tecumseh Sherman.

The North had too much power for the South. It could build the ships to blockade southern ports. It had the food to feed its armies and the people at home. Year by year, it seized control of important rivers— the Ohio, Tennessee, Cumberland, Mississippi—so that the Confederacy was squeezed into a little stockade from which the only escape was surrender.

All through those terrible years no one in America suffered more than Abraham Lincoln. He fought the war up to the hilt, intending to win, and yet he felt no bitterness toward the South. As the years of torment mounted, he grew deeply religious, believing that slavery always had been a sin for which the country was being punished and telling the people: "Yet, if God wills that it continues, until all wealth piled by the bondman's two hundred and fifty years of unrequited toil shall be sunk, and until every drop of blood drawn with a lash, shall be paid by

another drawn by the sword, as was said three thousand years ago, so still it must be said, 'The judgments of the Lord are true and righteous altogether.'"

A sense of failure also grew in Lincoln and as November, 1864, approached he did not believe that he could be re-elected. Many counseled that an election should not be held, but Lincoln shook his head. If the people were not free to choose their own leaders, then there was no country. He won easily, failing only to carry the states of Maryland, Delaware and New Jersey—the people were more with him than he had believed.

So on a raw March day in 1865 he arose to deliver his Second Inaugural. The war must soon end — that he knew. Then, one nation again — what? He looked up at the bronze statue of Freedom that now crowned the dome of the Capitol. In his heart he realized there could be only one fair and honest answer. He spoke it fervently:

"With malice toward none; with charity for all; with firmness in the right, as God gives us to see the right, let us strive on to finish the work we are in; to bind up the nation's wounds; to care for him who shall have borne the battle, and for his widow and his orphan—to do all which may achieve and cherish a just and lasting peace, among ourselves, and with all nations."

On Palm Sunday Lee and Grant met at Appomattox Court House and agreed, as gentlemen and countrymen, upon terms of surrender. The North rejoiced and the South, with good cause, wept for its honored dead who had died in vain. In the twisted mind of John Wilkes Booth, an actor, the grief snapped the last resource of sanity. A few nights later he crept up the stairs in Ford's Theater to the box where the President sat. He shot Mr. Lincoln in the back of the head.

Next morning the President died—a beloved friend to the people of the North, a true friend to the people of the South who now so badly needed understanding, trust, and kind leadership.

ANDREW JOHNSON

"A Man Without a Party"

STUNNED and bewildered, people walked the streets, mourning the death of Lincoln. Later when the funeral train of the Great Emancipator made its sad, solemn journey to Springfield, Illinois, crowds gathered along the tracks and men bared their heads and women wept in a final tribute to the President who had led the nation through four years of bloody civil strife.

In their grief, the people vaguely realized that Andrew Johnson had been sworn into office as seventeenth President of the United States. He was no Lincoln, a good many said bitterly. In fact, he was not even a Republican, and since no self-respecting Southern Democrat would offer him house room, he came to power "a man without a party." Those who hated him most declared that he was an habitual drunkard, which was untrue.

But Andy Johnson was a fighter—something that the people, and most of all the Radical Republicans who now controlled Congress, soon discovered. A desperate, unremitting struggle against long odds really had been the sum of the new President's life since that twenty-ninth day of December, 1808, when he had been born to poor but proud parents in Raleigh, North Carolina. At the age of four young Andy had watched his father die from injuries sustained in rescuing another man from drowning and in his tenth year the boy had begun to earn his own livelihood as an apprentice to a tailor.

A craving to learn gnawed at young Andy. Fellow workmen taught the boy his alphabet and, borrowing a book, he learned how to read. A great day in Andy's life came in May, 1826, when with his mother and stepfather he drove a two-wheel cart, drawn by a blind pony, into the little town of Greeneville, Tennessee. Here he met a fine, sensitive girl, Eliza McCardle, who became his wife. Eliza taught him how to write and read aloud to him while Andy sat plying his needle.

Landholders in those days ran politics in Tennessee and even the state constitution protected their interests. In Greeneville young Johnson set out to dispute the political supremacy of this "aristocratic coterie" and to the surprise of many — perhaps his own included — was twice elected town alderman and then mayor. Thus began in 1828 the long and often stormy political career that saw Johnson in turn elected to the State Legislature, to Congress, to the Governorship of Tennessee, and to the Senate.

One thing could always be counted on with Andy — he thought for himself and spoke his own mind. He supported the Kansas-Nebraska Bill as ardently as any Southern Democrat and campaigned for the pro-slavery Breckinridge over Lincoln in the election of 1860, yet when the southern states began to dissolve the Union, he came roaring out of Tennessee like an angry warrior. Southerners neither soon forgot nor forgave the speech he hurled at the secessionists:

"I would have them arrested and tried for treason, and if convicted,

Stanley Dersh

by the eternal God, they should suffer the penalty of the law at the hands of the executioner."

Returning to Tennessee after this speech, Andy was assaulted by a mob at Liberty, Virginia, intent on taking the law into their hands as far as he was concerned. Andy whipped out a pistol and told his attackers to come ahead. He escaped, but all along the way home crowds hissed him and he was burned or hung in effigy in many southern communities.

Andrew Johnson retained his seat in the Senate until 1862 when President Lincoln appointed him military governor of Tennessee. He reached Nashville on March twelfth and six days later in a proclamation offered "a full and competent amnesty for all past acts and declarations" to any person taking an oath of allegiance to the national government. This willingness in Andy to forget and forgive the past was a trait that his enemies in the North remembered and his enemies in the South ignored.

Meanwhile Andy proved to be a vigorous wartime governor. He had the courage of a lion, a characteristic that was largely instrumental in holding Nashville against a Confederate force. During his administration twenty-five regiments enlisted to fight for the Union, and though he never hesitated to throw any "traitor" into jail, he was a moderate, discreet governor whose actions strengthened tremendously Union sentiment in Tennessee.

When the time came to renominate Lincoln for President, the convention believed that in fair recognition of the political sacrifices made by the War Democrats in behalf of the Union they should have the second place on the ticket. Johnson became the man chosen—not a Republican like Lincoln, but more like Lincoln than most Republicans.

And that was the trouble. Lincoln, in his Second Inaugural, could preach the fine belief that the war should end "with malice toward none, with charity for all," but very few Radical Republicans wished to have it end that way. Should the North be too quick to forget and forgive,

then the Radical Republicans, who were really a political minority under normal circumstances, could lose control of the government to Southern Democrats. Moreover, Northern industrialists, who, by supporting the Radical Republicans had grown fat on high tariffs, a national banking system, large grants of land from the public domain and freedom from governmental interference with business, saw these privileges endangered if the South regained its political power. So these two groups, working in harness, made revenge on the "traitors" their national battle-cry.

Johnson stood against this attitude. To the southern states he said, first, repeal your ordinances of secession. Next, he said, ratify the Thirteenth Amendment, prohibiting slavery. State and Confederate debts arising from the war, he believed, should be forgotten. Except for a group of leaders directly responsible for the rebellion, he offered amnesty with the restoration of full civil liberties and property (slaves excepted) to anyone taking an oath of future loyalty. All who received amnesty, he declared, should be entitled to vote or to hold office.

Johnson's policies, which carried out the spirit of Lincoln's ideas on reconstruction, impressed the Radical Republicans as representing a menace about as bad as the bubonic plague. Against Johnson's opposition, they demanded that the right to vote be given immediately to the Negro—the right to vote Republican, of course. Democrats, as a group, were branded as belonging to the party of treason. Fear and hatred in any form that would stir up support for the Radical Republicans was employed. Upon a South defeated but still proud—its plantations looted, its railroads damaged, its economy ruined—descended arrogant, shameful carpetbaggers with Northern soldiers to back up their rule.

With the Radical Republicans in control of Congress, Johnson's only means of fighting the foolish, vindictive laws that were passed was by exercising his right of veto. The Radical Republicans overrode his vetoes, passed a law that limited the power of the President over the army though the Constitution made him its Commander-in-chief, and even passed legislation that prevented the President from dismissing his own subordinate executives!

Still not satisfied, in 1868 impeachment proceedings were begun against Johnson for the heinous "crime"—at least this was the only charge against him ever proved—of disagreeing with Congress! On May sixteenth the Senate made its test vote on impeachment—thirty-five for conviction, nineteen for acquittal, or only one vote short of the two-thirds majority necessary to impeach!

To say that Andrew Johnson always kept his head or held his tongue in this crisis would not be true. Yet, in some respects, the honest motives and even the nobility of a President have never been so thoroughly misunderstood or misrepresented. Perhaps Lincoln's personality and popularity would have enabled him to carry out policies similar to those that Johnson advocated. Or perhaps he, too, would have become the whipping boy of the Radical Republicans.

When Johnson's term ended, he returned to Tennessee. Once he ran for the Senate and once for Congress without success, then in 1875 the people of the state seemed to remember their old affection for him and elected him to the Senate. On July twenty-ninth, visiting his daughter in Carter's Station, Tennessee, he was stricken with paralysis and died two days later. He was buried in Greeneville where the self-educated tailor had once surprised everyone by becoming a town alderman.

ULYSSES S. GRANT

"The Uncommon Common Man"

ALMOST EVERYONE lives with a secret, and Ulysses S. Grant had his. The birth certificate that proved he was born April 27, 1822 in Point Pleasant, Ohio, revealed that his first name was Hiram. And "Hiram" Grant he remained for seventeen years.

Grant's father ran a tannery and the boy hated the smell of the place as much as he loved the horses in the stable. Often his parents were horrified by the sight of the child, scarcely past the age of a toddler, weaving between the legs or under the bellies of horses. He possessed no fear of the animals towering over him, and from the time he was old enough to sit on a horse he could ride like the wind.

His education was gained at various subscription schools. "I was not studious in habit," he remembered, "and probably did not make progress enough to compensate for the outlay for board and tuition." He never forgot the procession of teachers who kept him repeating: "A noun is the name of a thing." In time he was willing to believe it!

113

From early childhood, Grant's good-humored, easy-going disposition was the trait that impressed everyone. Whether attending school or chopping wood or doing household chores or fishing or swimming, he remained even-tempered and affable. He could not recall a time when his parents scolded or punished him.

Not that Grant didn't have queer quirks. Any backward step made him feel dizzy so that he was, by nature, a go-ahead fellow. Prodded by an itchy foot, he liked to travel by himself and at fifteen had been on journeys as far as seventy miles from home. Two years later he received the appointment to West Point that he didn't want—but he went anyway, to please his father. At least through a mistake he was entered on the rolls as "U. S." Grant and was rid of "Hiram" forever. Fellow cadets nicknamed him "Uncle Sam," then shortened that to Sam.

Many congressmen believed that operating West Point was a waste of money and threatened to close it down. Grant hoped that they would. He spent much of his time reading novels, thought he would like to teach mathematics (his best subject), and had no desire whatever to be a soldier. But Congress failed him and West Point remained open. A slight case of consumption was his next hope of escaping the army, but he recovered—thanks mainly to the outdoor life forced upon him— and when the Mexican War broke out he found himself in the thick of it.

To Grant's own surprise, he made a good soldier! Yet at the first sound of a hostile gun, Grant confessed: "I felt sorry that I had enlisted." But the dash and flair of the Grant who one day would rank among the great generals in history were revealed in the Battle of Monterey. The American forces desperately needed ammunition and Grant volunteered to secure it.

The way to make this ride, Grant knew, was like a Comanche. With only one foot holding to the cantle of the saddle, and an arm over the neck of the horse, he clung to the side of the animal not exposed to the enemy. At a full run, Grant started. Mexican bullets splattered the ground. Chuckling, Grant slid to the ground when he reached the safety of a blockhouse. He wasn't even scratched.

Grant was married now. He had to think of supporting a family. Still, all he knew was soldiering, so he remained in the army after the Mexican War. When he was shipped finally to service in far-off California, his homesickness grew into melancholy and he decided that anything was better than separation from his family. He resigned and came back to Missouri to build a new life.

He did not do well at farming. Sometimes, to eke out a living, he drove a wagonload of wood to St. Louis. At last Grant faced the bitter truth. Though he hated his father's leather business, he had no choice but to join his brothers in it. He loaded his family on a steamer and sailed to Galena, Illinois, where the family business was now located. Loafers at the dock saw a short, squat man, chewing the stump of a cigar, slouch down the gangplank. He still wore the tattered army coat. All that anyone could say for him was that he had a wart on his cheek—like old Abe Lincoln.

It was hard to imagine a more commonplace fellow than Ulysses S. Grant. In time, when people understood the clear mind behind his quiet smile and his ability to think through a problem and come up with the unexpected—and *right*—answer, then they knew, as a friend once said, that Grant was "the uncommon common man."

As a general in the Civil War, Grant started slowly. No one seemed to believe he could be trusted with a fighting army. He was pushed off to unimportant posts, almost forgotten, his advice ignored. But Grant had ideas about war. "When in doubt, fight," he said, which was more than most Union generals were doing. The army that hit first, seizing the initiative, usually won — and on this belief he began to act until at Vicksburg in the spring and summer of 1863 he emerged as a great general and perhaps the North's best general.

Grant won at Vicksburg because he believed in himself and took a chance. Other generals insisted that they must operate from a base of supplies, but Grant said no—he would live off the country as he fought. Thus he unbalanced the Confederate defenders of Vicksburg, and before they guessed what he was doing, he sliced in between two rebel armies and had them both in his pocket. The same audacity won for him in Tennessee a year later, and then Lincoln called him to the White House to make him a lieutenant general in command of all Union armies.

Many chuckled when they saw that pair together—the tall, gangling President beaming down at the stump of a general. But Lincoln knew that he had found a commander who might be a match for the valiant, hitherto unbeatable Lee. Grant had pluck, a willingness to keep on fighting even when the battle went against him, and overwhelming resources of men and material. In time these advantages should tell—and in time they did tell so that on an April Sunday in 1865 Grant and Lee met to shake hands and put a stop to this brothers' quarrel. When Union troops started to fire guns in celebration, Grant stopped the demonstration at once. He knew how gallant the foe had been. Like Lincoln, he had reached the climax of the war with an unembittered heart.

A nation still misunderstanding Andrew Johnson turned naturally to its war hero at the next election. Nominated by the Republicans, Grant won easily, carrying twenty-six states and piling up a popular vote of 3,015,071 against eight states and a vote of 2,709,613 for his Democratic opponent. Mississippi, Texas and Virginia did not vote in the election, and many claimed that Grant also would have carried New York except for fraudulent votes.

In this charge was the clue to the eight troubled years that faced Grant in the White House. Not only were carpetbaggers ruining the South, but elsewhere graft ruled government and business. This was the age of Boss Tweed in New York City when a public building worth $250,000 cost taxpayers $10,000,000 through dishonest contracts, when unscrupulous speculators like Jim Fisk and Jay Gould sold millions of

dollars of worthless stock, and when an effort to buy up the gold reserve produced Black Friday and brought the nation to the brink of financial disaster.

In such times the affable, pitifully inexperienced Grant fumbled from one crisis to another. His effort to annex Santo Domingo was rejected in the Senate. The corruption in government encouraged a small wing of liberal Republicans—ridiculed by the "Spoils System" gang as Mugwumps—to push for civil service reforms. The "Salary Grab Bill of 1873" raised Federal salaries, including a boost of from $25,000 to $50,000 a year for the President. The positive accomplishments during Grant's administration—the adoption of the Fifteenth Amendment, the establishment of Yellowstone National Park, the completion of the first transcontinental railroad, and the admission of Colorado into the Union — were dimmed by the rising cry against fraud in government. Unfairly Grant was accused of being implicated in the gold scheme that brought on Black Friday and the Panic of 1873.

Two months after leaving the White House, Grant made a tour of the world and everywhere was received with high honors. He hoped to run again for President, but the liberals within his own party — those Mugwumps — were too strong for him now. Going into the banking business with Ferdinand Ward, mismanagement of the firm by Grant's partners led in 1884 to his complete financial ruin.

Penniless now, dying of cancer of the throat, the old general fought his last great battle. He would finish writing his memoirs before he died and so recoup his fortunes. Visitors to Saratoga, New York, where Grant had a summer home, saw the sick old man sitting on a porch in shawl and stocking-cap, pitting himself against death. As though a schoolboy back in Ohio, he said: "A verb is anything that signifies to be, to do, to suffer. I signify all three." Thousands passed by to see him, to wave, to let him know how much they still admired him. One week before he died on July 23, 1885 he completed his memoirs — a victor to the end!

RUTHERFORD B. HAYES

"And Lemonade Lucy"

AFTER the scandals of the Grant administrations, the exposure of political shysters like Boss Tweed who were stealing the gold out of the teeth of taxpayers, and the shenanigans of unprincipled financiers who had produced Black Friday, a great spirit of reform swept the country. The Democratic nominee for President was the wealthy, socially prominent, incorruptible Samuel J. Tilden of New York. Let the Republicans try and find his match, crowed the Democrats.

The Republicans did. In fact, they went a step further. Their candidate was not only wealthy, socially prominent, a distinguished lawyer, a former congressman and Governor of Ohio, but also a Civil War hero. From that fourth day of October, 1822, when Rutherford B. Hayes drew his first breath in Delaware, Ohio, contended the Republicans, his life had been without a flaw. But it is a poor politician who cannot find some mud to sling, and the Democrats did not fail in the case of Hayes.

In the end they accused him—and not without some justification—of stealing the Presidency.

Actually Hayes's backers rather than he bore the responsibility for the political highjinks that marked the election of 1876. The character of Hayes was as unimpeachable as his friends insisted. As an earnest young man, he had been a conscientious, brilliant student at Kenyon College and Harvard University—so much so that in his diary at Harvard, when he became lame from playing ball, he chided himself: "Pretty business for a law student."

As a lawyer, Hayes was tremendously successful, winning special acclaim for his handling of criminal cases. And as a lifelong opponent of slavery, Hayes threw his full heart into the conflict that divided the Union. It was not without good reason that he rose to the rank of brigadier general and won commendation from Grant. His gallantry in the battle at South Mountain in September, 1862, was typical of his fighting caliber. Severely wounded in his left arm, he led his men in a bloody charge until he collapsed and was carried from the field. Typical also of his devotion to the Union was his reaction in 1864 when he was nominated for Congress and friends urged him to resign from the army so that he could campaign for himself.

"An officer fit for duty, who at this crisis would abandon his post to electioneer for a seat in Congress, ought to be scalped," Hayes retorted firmly.

But it was the other candidate who was scalped—Hayes won the seat without electioneering. In Congress after the war, like so many Whigs who had been reborn as Republicans, Hayes slavishly followed the party line, denouncing any repudiation of the war debt in the South and supporting the impeachment of Andrew Johnson. His terms as Governor of Ohio came afterward, and looking at the Grant administrations from afar, he began to sense keenly where public sentiment was going. The North was growing weary, perhaps even conscience-stricken,

OUR CHOICE

over the military domination of the South. The country, sick of corruption in government, liked the movement for civil-service legislation started by the Mugwumps. And after the Panic of 1873 the people wanted a sound currency with the government standing behind every greenback.

To these three objectives, Hayes added the stipulation that under no circumstances would he serve more than one term as President. Then the two parties, with their incorruptible candidates in the field, proceeded to make the campaign of 1876 as dirty a name-calling contest as the country ever had seen. On the morning after the election, the result gave Tilden a popular vote of 4,300,590 and an electoral vote of 196 against a popular vote for Hayes of 4,036,298 and an electoral vote of 173.

The Republicans would not concede defeat. Unlawful, strong-arm tactics in Louisiana, South Carolina and Florida, they charged, had kept Negroes from going to the polls. The election, referred to a special committee of Congress, hinged now on one of the most brazen deals in history. Hayes did not know what was going on, but Republicans promised Southern Democrats in the three contested states that if they would throw their electoral vote to Hayes, Federal troops would be withdrawn and the states could control their own affairs. Fifty-six hours before the inauguration of the nineteenth President of the United States, the bargain was consummated and Hayes declared the winner!

Moreover, the bargain was kept, the Negroes were deprived of their vote and white supremacy returned to the solid South. Federal appointments on the basis of merit rather than party loyalty badly crimped the old spoils system. Over Hayes's veto, silver was made the currency supporting greenbacks, giving farmers the "cheap" dollar they wanted, but gold supported bank notes. The country's financial confidence gradually returned, in good part because crop disasters in Europe were matched by bumper crops in America in 1879.

But strife came first, and a new shadow fell upon the country. Labor organizations like the Knights of Labor, the Trainmen's Union and the

Molly Maguires in the hard-coal industry were growing stronger. Hard times following the Panic of 1873 had made industrial workers rebellious and resentful. In 1877 a series of wage cuts touched off an explosion.

Beginning in Martinsburg, West Virginia a strike by the Trainmen's Union spread to Pittsburgh and other cities of the Midwest. At one time as many as one hundred thousand men were reported out on strike. Riots were frequent and property damage grew enormous as the country's transportation system was paralyzed by what the press called the Great Railroad Strike. State militia, when they responded to the call to subdue these disturbances, mixed in bloody battles with the trainmen. Railroad owners in West Virginia, Maryland and Pennsylvania appealed to President Hayes for help, and Federal troops quickly restored order.

Life in the White House underwent many changes while Hayes lived there. His wife, the former Lucy Webb, became known as "Lemonade Lucy" because she refused to serve intoxicating drinks. There was a rumor that rum was added to the punch on the sly, but President Hayes chuckled at these stories. He had added rum *flavoring* to fool those who thought they were fooling him! Another custom that his wife brought to Washington was the annual egg-roll on the White House lawn.

The age was one in America when boys read the stories of Horatio Alger, Jr. until their eyes were bloodshot, when the Pullman Company constructed its first "hotel" on wheels, and when Alexander Graham Bell invented the telephone. President Hayes called Bell to the White House to demonstrate the new wonder and promptly ordered a telephone installed. Another visitor to the White House was Thomas A. Edison, who played his new phonograph and so fascinated the President that they talked until after three o'clock in the morning.

When Hayes's term ended, he returned to Fremont, Ohio, to spend quiet years with his books and in such public work as serving as President of the National Prison Association and the Peabody Education Fund. Death came to him gently on January 17, 1893.

JAMES A. GARFIELD

"The Last Log Cabin President"

JAMES A. GARFIELD was the last President of the United States to begin life in a log cabin. Cuyahoga County, in Ohio, where Garfield was born on November 19, 1831, was part of that land largely settled by families from Connecticut known as "The Wilderness" and the "Western Reserve." His father, Abram Garfield, died suddenly, leaving his mother to raise four small children. James was the youngest.

To say that the Garfields struggled against poverty and trying times was to stretch a point. Who didn't on that frontier? And the Garfields, as devout members of a religious sect called the Campbellites, accepted adversity cheerfully. A Campbellite interpreted the Scriptures simply, as any plain man would read them. To be pleasing in the eyes of the Lord, a Campbellite believed, a man should enjoy hard, honest toil and think for himself.

James met both these tests of a good Campbellite. Going to school

124

in a log hut, he learned to read at the age of three, and as far as anyone could tell he never stopped reading thereafter—anything that came into his hands, although works of history were his special delight. By fourteen he was a strong lad worthy of his hire on any neighborhood farm, a good student who displayed aptitude for arithmetic and grammar, and his reading of adventure stories made him yearn for a life at sea.

So on a day in 1848 he arrived in Cleveland, intending to ship aboard a schooner as a sailor. One look around the vessel, however, took away all appetite for that venture, yet pride prevented him from admitting defeat and returning home. Without money, he had to find a job somewhere, and settled on driving mules along the tow-path of the Ohio Canal.

Rough and tumble was the life of a canal-man in that age when America was creating the legend of Mike Fink. Canal justice was the law of a quick pair of fists. Canal-men worked, lived, cussed, and drank hard—scarcely an environment suited to an earnest young Campbellite. But James Garfield withstood the hard knocks, and perhaps handed back a few. He was promoted from the tow-path to handling a boat. In a canal-man's language, that was "heating the old tin oven."

James never could learn enough. Working as a carpenter and a farm hand, he spent a term at Geagua Seminary in Chester, Ohio, earning a dividend on this toil by falling in love with Lucretia Rudolph, the girl he would one day marry. From Chester in 1851 he went to the Hiram Eclectic Institute (now Hiram College), where he paid his expenses by teaching English and ancient languages and saved enough to give himself the final polish of an "eastern education." Like a professor solving a problem in algebra, he studied the best features of Yale, Brown and Williams and decided on the latter institution. In 1856 he graduated from Williams with the highest honors in his class.

At that commencement, had the seniors voted on the member of their class most likely to succeed, their unanimous choice would have been James A. Garfield. And they would have been right. In the next

six crowded years Garfield became a college president (at Hiram), a
state senator, a major general in the Union army, and a member-elect
of Congress.

In the war Garfield was particularly distinguished in the campaign
that cleared Kentucky of the Rebels. Like Grant, he was a commander
who would take a risk when he had thought through a plan. West Point-
trained General Humphrey Marshall led some five thousand Confederate
troops in Kentucky and Garfield was lucky if he could count half that
number. Moreover Marshall had dug into mountainous country where
the people were openly hostile to the Union.

Undaunted, Garfield played the game of a terrier nipping at the heels
of an antagonist until he caught the annoyed Marshall separated from his

base of supplies. Garfield's boys struck in a vicious hand-to-hand battle that lasted five hours. Then reinforcements reached the outnumbered Union boys. Marshall was licked.

Elected to Congress while the war was still in progress, Garfield was urged by both President Lincoln and Secretary of War Stanton to resign from the army since level-headed fighters were as much needed in the Government as on the battlefield. So at the age of thirty-two Garfield began his career as a congressman, and in succeeding years became known as the champion of the "hard-money" men. He would yield no quarter against those who wished to water down the national currency. Yet when fellow Republicans in 1870 attached to his appropriation bill amendments that authorized the army to supervise elections in the South, Garfield cried out at this constitutional injustice. Perhaps many Republicans didn't like his rebellion, but the people of Ohio did. They sent him to the Senate.

Garfield came to Chicago for the Republican Convention in 1880 with only one thought in mind—to stop Grant in his bid for a third term as President. The contest for the nomination quickly settled into a long, bitter struggle among Grant, James G. Blaine of Maine and Elihu Washburne of Illinois. On the thirty-fourth ballot, in an effort to break the monotony, came an unexpected announcement:

"Wis-con-sin casts thirty-six votes for James A. Garfield."

People laughed. Two ballots later they were cheering as the anti-Grant forces broke rank and united behind "dark horse" Garfield to make him the candidate. In the election against General Winfield Scott Hancock, the Democratic nominee, Garfield's plurality was only 9,464 out of a popular vote of more than 9,000,000.

The President who, like the Horatio Alger, Jr. heroes of that time, had worked his way up from rags to riches, had the pleasant surprise at his inauguration of seeing a group of former Confederate soldiers break through the crowd on Pennsylvania Avenue and rush forward, waving the national flag in a symbol that the wounds of the war had healed.

That summer of 1881, when the country talked of Tuskegee Institute that Booker T. Washington had opened and the American Red Cross that Clara Barton had organized, the big news from Washington was the drag-down fight Garfield was waging with professional politicians over Federal appointments. The politicians groaned and the people cheered, for Garfield was too unflinchingly honest to budge on a principle.

In good spirits, knowing the country respected him, on a day in early July the President set off to deliver the commencement address at Williams College. Arm in arm with Blaine, now his Secretary of State, he was passing through the waiting room of the Baltimore and Potomac station when a bearded, clearly demented man stepped forth. His name was Charles J. Guiteau, and his eyes were murky with anger over the stream of unanswered letters he had sent Garfield seeking appointment as a consul to France. Raising a little English bulldog pistol, Guiteau fired two shots.

The second bullet, entering Garfield's back, fractured a rib and lodged deep in his body. The inventor of the telephone, Alexander Graham Bell, was rushed to the White House in the vain hope that with a special electrical device he could locate the bullet. For ten weeks the President lay stricken while the nation prayed and showered him with gifts. In September he was moved to the pleasant climate of the little New Jersey seashore town of Elberon. At first he seemed to improve, but in mid-month symptoms of blood-poisoning developed. On September 19th he lapsed into unconsciousness and died peacefully.

Booth, the assassin of Lincoln, had died in the barn where Federal troops cornered him and Guiteau, the assassin of Garfield, was captured, tried and hanged in Washington on June 30, 1882. By then Garfield's body had been borne to Cleveland to rest in a beautiful cemetery overlooking Lake Erie, where once the excited eyes of James A. Garfield searched among schooner masts in a boyhood dream of high adventure.

Stanley Dersh

CHESTER A. ARTHUR

"The Gentleman Boss"

FOR THE FOURTH TIME in history the American people were forced to become acquainted with a man they had never expected to make President. "The gentleman boss," many characterized Chester Alan Arthur, intending no compliment. Wasn't he, after all, a product of the New York State political machine that had been involved in some of the worst scandals of the Grant administrations? Why had he been nominated on the same ticket with Garfield except that he seemed to represent a safe sop to the Grant forces in an effort to secure party harmony? And now Chester Alan Arthur was the twenty-first President of the United States!

"Ye gods!" muttered liberal Republicans, realizing how fate had tricked them.

What critics forgot, of course, was the fact that when on October 5, 1830 Arthur had greeted the world in the Vermont town of Fairfield, he had entered the family of a distinguished clergyman. A tough moral fiber had been woven into his character. In addition, he was as bright as a new penny. A chap didn't graduate from Union College a member of Phi Beta Kappa, a scholastic honorary society, unless he had brains. At the age of eighteen, a chap didn't become principal of the academy at North Pownal, Vermont without a good head on his shoulders.

One person who could have told the country that Chester A. Arthur could stand by a principle was Lizzie Jennings, but of course no one asked Lizzie. One year as a schoolmaster had been enough for Arthur, and he had come to New York City to establish himself as a lawyer. There in 1855 he became interested in Lizzie, a Negro Sunday School superintendent who one Sabbath was put off a trolley car. At that time the city's streetcar companies made a practice of excluding Negroes from their vehicles and provided no separate system of transportation for them.

Arthur, who had inherited a strong dislike for slavery from his clergyman-father, now took the next step by fighting for equal civil rights for the Negro race. He sued the streetcar company in behalf of Lizzie, won a judgment, and for years the Colored People's Legal Rights Association celebrated the anniversary of his victory in court.

Arthur's success in law mounted steadily and brought him an intimate friendship with Edwin D. Morgan, the Governor of New York. Appointed the state's Quartermaster-General during the Civil War, he made a distinguished record in this office and likewise rose steadily in political influence under the guidance of the state's Republican boss, Senator Roscoe Conkling. Arthur was a stanch Grant-for-President organizer in 1870 and his reward, when Grant won, was appointment as Collector of the Port of New York.

During Arthur's control, it was an open question whether the New York Customs House belonged to the Federal Government or the Republican Party. Certainly prominent state Republican leaders could be found holding the chief customs house jobs and doubtless some fines that were collected went to the party instead of the Federal Treasury.

Rutherford B. Hayes, cleaning out the unsavory gang that had latched onto the too-innocent Grant, ousted Chester A. Arthur with the rest. And now by the foul luck of an assassin's bullet this same boss-controlled Arthur was himself President! With little wonder reformers, beholding the tall, handsome, immaculately attired Arthur taking the oath of office, blinked their eyes and growled, "Heaven save us!"

Perhaps Heaven did. Those who wanted to ridicule Chester A. Arthur as a fop who fancied himself could point to the first tiled bathroom that he installed in the White House. But in the exciting years that followed—years that witnessed the completion of the Brooklyn Bridge, the organization of the American Federation of Labor, the adoption of a system of standard time, the dedication of the Washington Monument and a flood of dime novels from the presses of that prodigious publisher, Erastus F. Beadle—the greatest excitement was how Arthur turned his back on the political bosses and ran a completely honest government!

Senator Conkling, ex-President Grant—no one could budge Arthur in his resolution to make appointments only on what he considered were the merits of candidates. On January 16, 1883 he signed the Pendleton Civil Service Act and appointed its author, Dorman B. Eaton, chairman of the first Civil Service Commission. He cleaned up the Post Office Department to prevent future frauds and ordered party officials to avoid seeking graft for future campaign funds. When the professional politicians sought to create a new "pork barrel" for themselves in a Rivers and Harbors Bill that provided for numerous unnecessary expenditures, Arthur promptly killed the measure with a veto. He tried also to defeat the Chinese Exclusion Bill barring immigrants from China from coming into the country, but in this instance Congress had the votes to pass the legislation over the President's veto.

A widower who every day placed a fresh bouquet beside the picture of his dead wife, Arthur exemplified the sense of duty to the people that raised occupancy of the White House above party loyalty. He enjoyed his role as rather a lone-wolf crusader and wanted another four years at it. Since he had stepped squarely on the toes of Senator Conkling, the President felt impelled to build his own political machine in New York, and in the gubernatorial contest in 1882 forced upon the Republicans the candidacy of Charles J. Folger, his Secretary of the Treasury.

But the Democrats that year had a powerful candidate who not only defeated Folger (thereby tremendously diminishing Arthur's political prestige), but of whom a great deal more soon would be heard. His name was Grover Cleveland. Still, Arthur tried for renomination at the next national convention. When on the first ballot he drew only a few votes, he knew that his political goose had been cooked. The nomination went to James G. Blaine.

Arthur retired to private life in New York City. On November 18, 1886 he suffered a stroke of apoplexy. His sudden death stunned the country. With affection the people remembered "The Gentleman Boss" who had proved to be first of all a gentleman of unimpeachable integrity. The Civil Service Act, restoring honor to Federal service, still endures as his monument.

GROVER CLEVELAND

"The Veto President"

BECAUSE GROVER CLEVELAND learned how to say no, he holds a unique place in American history. Elected our twenty-second President, he was defeated, then re-elected our twenty-fourth President, an achievement never equaled. "Whatever you say, tell the truth," he once warned his campaign managers. If anyone wanted proof that honesty is the best policy, he needed to look no farther than the political career of Grover Cleveland.

Like Chester A. Arthur, Cleveland was born into a clergyman's family at Caldwell, New Jersey on March 18, 1837. The lad was named Stephen Grover, in honor of another clergyman, but early dropped the "Stephen." Among his ancestors was Moses Cleveland, who came to America in 1635 and gave his name to the great Ohio city on the shores of Lake Erie.

With a family of nine children to support, the Reverend Mr. Cleveland found the life of a country minister a difficult one. Grover's principal boyhood memory was of a family on the move—from Caldwell to the New York towns of Fayetteville, Clinton and Holland Point—as his father tried to establish himself in a community that could better provide for his numerous clan. Grover clerked for a time in a store, then packed his belongings and journeyed to New York City where an older brother secured a position for him as a clerk and assistant teacher in an institution for the blind.

Grover knew he was not getting ahead. The memory of the distinguished ancestor, after whom a flourishing city was named, inspired him to turn westward in search of a brighter future. On the way he stopped off at Black Rock (now part of Buffalo, New York) where an uncle persuaded him to help with the compilation of the "American Herd-Book." Grover seemed to know at once that Buffalo was the place for him. The year was 1855, and that autumn he secured a position with the law firm of Rogers, Bowen & Rogers. His wages were not magnificent—four dollars a week—but he could study Blackstone and other legal authorities and four years later was admitted to the practice of law.

Like most Presidents, little in Grover's early years gave promise of future distinction. He was cheerful, conscientious, ambitious, hard-working—exactly like thousands of other young men in Buffalo. In 1863 he was appointed assistant district attorney of Erie County—but where in the United States could you find a well-populated county that didn't have an assistant district attorney? He was named sheriff—but there were thousands of sheriffs.

And yet there *was* a difference. People in Erie County talked about it. In executing murderers, other sheriffs gave the unhappy assignment to an assistant. Sheriff Grover Cleveland refused to pass an unpleasant duty to another. He sprung the trap on the gallows that sent a pair of condemned cutthroats to their deaths.

Stanley Dersh

Still, little else in Grover Cleveland's record set him apart. He was a successful lawyer rather than a brilliant one, a small-town politician rather than influential leader. And in his background was one political liability, for during the Civil War he had borrowed $150 to hire a substitute to fight for him. True, the law allowed him to do so, but people talked anyway. Yet Cleveland was scrupulously honest, and with the Republicans tarred by the black brushes of many political scandals, the Democrats decided in 1881 to run him for mayor of Buffalo.

Cleveland won easily and soon gained renown as "the veto mayor." In the first six months, by simply saying no to extravagant proposals, Cleveland saved the city $1,000,000—including $500 for a Fourth of July celebration, for which he could find no legal authority. In 1882, in one of the quickest rises in political history, he became "the veto governor" of New York. Among the bills he turned down was one providing for a five-cent streetcar fare, an action that brought him into a head-on political collision with a young Republican senator named Theodore Roosevelt. But Cleveland maintained that the bill violated a contract with the streetcar companies and was therefore illegal. Personally he would be glad to be rid of the ten-cent fare!

To everyone's surprise, two years later "the veto governor" became "the veto president," in a campaign marked by rank vilification that reached its limit when, at a Blaine rally in New York, a clergyman cried that a vote for Cleveland was a vote for "Rum, Romanism, and Rebellion." This gentleman succeeded in swinging enough Catholic votes behind Cleveland to give him a popular plurality over Blaine of 62,683 and a victory in the electoral vote of 219 to 182.

Cleveland was now a massive man with a bull-neck who weighed 260 pounds. He moved slowly and thought slowly, and settled his mind as he settled in a chair, refusing to change his position without a terrible struggle. "We love him for the enemies he has made," said a Wisconsin delegate in nominating Cleveland, and in his first four stormy years in

Washington "the veto president" succeeded in increasing their number.

Farm income was low, prices of manufactures high, the laboring man hard-pinched to make ends meet. An incident occurred in Chicago in 1886 that revealed the seething unrest of the people. On May Day the Knights of Labor called a mass meeting in Haymarket Square to rally its members to strike for an eight-hour day. Although eight anarchists later were condemned, the identity of the person who threw a bomb into the gathering was never established. One policeman was killed and others wounded.

The "Haymarket Riot" was a symbol like the Statue of Liberty which that fall was dedicated on Bedloe's Island in New York Harbor —America, the land of the free, was becoming a country where the poor could grow poorer. Cleveland, in his stoical, hard-headed way, did what he believed was right: He strengthened the Civil Service Act of 1883 and doubled the number of Federal employees it protected. He stood for a lower tariff to help the farmers and for "hard money" based on the gold standard to help industrialists. He signed into law the Interstate Commerce Act, allowing the Federal Government to regulate railroads and other systems of public transportation.

And he championed love, becoming the first President to be married in the White House. His bride, pretty, dark-eyed Frances Folsom of Buffalo, was twenty-seven years younger than Cleveland. The marriage ceremony took place in the Blue Room on a beautiful June day in 1886. A twenty-one gun salute in the Navy Yard ended the service.

Yet even Cupid couldn't make a restless country feel happy with the slow, methodical administration of Grover Cleveland. Actually he received more votes than his Republican opponent in 1888, but lost the electoral vote. Said the young Mrs. Cleveland on departing from the White House: "I want to find everything just as it is now when we come back...four years from today."

And back "the veto president" and his bride came! The country,

liking the policies of "Grover the Good" when it saw how much worse
the situation could become, re-elected him in a landslide. As twenty-
fourth President, Cleveland inherited a sick nation. Soon financial panic
would sweep the land. Farms by the thousands would be lost through
mortgage foreclosures. Bankrupt railroads, increasing labor disputes, a
Federal Treasury almost depleted of gold—these were some of the headaches that awaited Cleveland.

He quarreled with his own party over a high tariff bill, signed it
reluctantly because it provided for an income tax, then saw this pro-
vision struck down by the Supreme Court as unconstitutional.

The growing bitterness of labor unrest came to a climax in 1894 when strikers closed down the shops of the Pullman Company in the "company town" of Pullman, Illinois, near Chicago. The American Railway Union took up the cause of the strikers and all through the Middle and Far West boycotted trains to which Pullman cars were attached. An aggressive young leader, Eugene Debs, came to the fore.

Cleveland sided with management and capital. On the grounds that Government mails were being interrupted, Federal troops were sent to break the strike. Leaders like Debs were jailed, the Sherman Anti-trust Law was used to stop combinations in restraint of trade without recourse to trial by jury, and labor boycotts were declared illegal. Nearly 750,000 laborers suffered a mass defeat through the intervention of the Federal Government. Governor Altegeld of Illinois argued that Cleveland had ignored state rights in sending troops, and many legal authorities supported his view.

Clearly, a new battle line had been drawn that would affect the future of America. The great Columbian Exposition that had drawn 21,000,000 people to Chicago the year before to wonder at the 250,000 electric lamps illuminating the fair grounds, or the "horseless buggy" that Henry Ford drove through the streets of Detroit that year, or the admission of Utah to the Union two years later could not make hungry people forget what had happened. A father who sees a child shivering for lack of fuel does not argue legal technicalities reasonably.

Cleveland left the White House at the close of his second administration, a thoroughly unpopular man. He settled in Princeton, New Jersey, and again, on looking back, the people decided that he really had been "Grover the Good." Some said that he was our best President since Lincoln, and when death came on June 24, 1908 public sentiment had restored him to the favor he held in the election in 1892 when joyous Democrats had chanted:

"Grover! Grover! Four more years of Grover!
Out they go, in we go; then we'll be in clover!"

BENJAMIN HARRISON

"The Minority President"

EACH MORNING the electrician turned off the lights that had been burning all night in the White House. "The President's afraid to touch them," he told a friend, grinning. "He won't even push the buttons on the electric bells."

How quickly it became a custom in Washington to poke fun at Benjamin Harrison as the twenty-third President! To say that Harrison's critics enjoyed cutting him down to size was in itself a kind of joke, for the President barely measured five and a half feet. What the country soon suspected was that the man who occupied the White House in the middle of Cleveland's two terms had arrived there by catering to the "special interests" which had dominated the Republican Party since the presidential days of Grant.

The Republicans had made great capital out of the Harrison name, stressing the fact that on August 20, 1833 he had been born near

North Bend, Ohio on a farm that had belonged to his famous grandfather, William Henry Harrison, ninth President of the United States. The fact that his early training had been secured in a log schoolhouse gave the touch of an American political tradition that was rapidly vanishing. Thereafter he had attended Farmer's (now Belmont) College near Cincinnati and Miami University in Oxford, Ohio, married his college sweetheart and moved to Indianapolis to begin a career in law by serving as court crier for $2.50 a day. He was glad enough in those early days to take any case that might yield him a five-dollar fee, although half this sum usually went for hiring the horse and buggy that transported him to the scene of the trial.

A Whig turned Republican, Harrison served a term as city attorney and was elected reporter of the State Supreme Court before the outbreak of the war. Afterward a bid for the Governorship of Indiana that failed and a single term in the United States Senate were the principal political assets he carried to the convention which nominated him to oppose Cleveland in the campaign of 1888. Harrison received 100,000 less popular votes than Cleveland, but he won the electoral vote 233 to 169.

Harrison, "the minority president," cold and unimaginative in personality, served four chilly years in Washington. He was committed by his campaign to a high tariff and did not fail his backers. The Silver Purchase Act, intended to please silver-producing states and farmers, began the drain of gold from the Treasury that Cleveland inherited and the Pension Bill of 1890 gave a small pension to any veteran incapable of doing hard work. The overthrow of the Queen of Hawaii brought an appeal from that island for immediate annexation to the United States. Harrison sent a treaty to the Senate, favoring this action, but Cleveland later withdrew the treaty.

The country flexed its muscles against the aches of its growing pains during Harrison's four years in office. Six new states were admitted to the Union—Washington, Montana, North Dakota and South Dakota in 1889, Idaho and Wyoming in 1890—and the Oklahoma territory was opened for settlement. Meanwhile in the Sioux country the famous "Ghost Dance," incited by the belief that an Indian Christ would soon appear to return all the lands in the Dakotas to their original owners, kept that part of the nation in turmoil. The Federal cavalry finally caught up with Sitting Bull and his warriors in December of 1890 at the Battle of Wounded Knee. Some two hundred Indian men, women and children were massacred by the white soldiers in this last great pitched battle with the red man.

Another disaster that stunned the country occurred on May 31, 1889 when Conemaugh Dam, twelve miles above the city of Johnstown, Pennsylvania, gave way. The water of a lake two and a half miles long swept through the valley with terrible force. More than twenty-two hundred lives were lost.

Still, another kind of disaster, occurring in Homestead, Pennsylvania in 1892, foretold the trouble developing in the country that soon would engulf the political ambitions of Benjamin Harrison. A wage cut by the Carnegie Steel Company set off a strike. Three hundred armed men, rushed in to break the walk-out, locked in a bloody battle with the strikers and ten people were killed. Discontented farmers and workers thoroughly distrusted Benjamin Harrison as the candidate of "special interests." When the ballots were counted in the election of 1892, "the minority president" this time had also lost the electoral vote by a count of 145 to Cleveland's 277.

As quietly as Harrison had emerged from the shadows of a peaceful law practice in Indianapolis to become President, he now returned. His wife died in 1892 and he remarried four years later. He continued his active interest in politics and his fortunes as a lawyer increased. The Venezuelan Government enlisted his counsel in arbitrating a boundary dispute with England, his most conspicuous service in the years remaining before he died in Indianapolis on March 13, 1901.

144

WILLIAM McKINLEY

"Remember the Maine!"

WILLIAM JENNINGS BRYAN, the Democratic nominee for President in 1896, journeyed eighteen thousand miles to carry his campaign directly to the people. Everywhere thousands came to hear Bryan, "The Boy Orator of the Platte," as his golden tongue pleaded for an unlimited coinage of silver to expand the nation's currency and relieve the plight of the farmer in the West and the South. In contrast, the Republican candidate, William McKinley, conducted a quiet campaign from the front porch of his home in Canton, Ohio. He said simply that the country was prosperous, and that, in this era of "the full dinner pail," conservative policies were wisest.

The Democrats, of course, wielded their political brushes against the image of a calm, kindly, dignified McKinley. He stood for the "rule of the rich," they cried, and pointed to his patron and friend, powerful Mark Hanna, the multimillionaire political boss of Ohio, as evidence of whose interest McKinley would put first if he became the twenty-fifth President of the United States. A few who mocked his "front porch campaign" made a serious mistake. Years before Mrs. McKinley had become afflicted with epilepsy. A gentle, sensitive man, McKinley devoted every moment he could to caring for his wife, preferring to be a faithful husband to President if that became a necessary choice.

People liked McKinley for his steadfastness. Even though a rich political boss was behind his candidacy, McKinley's own origins had been modest and made him part of the great American majority. Born January 29, 1843 in Niles, Ohio, he had received an average education and was a junior at Allegheny College when poor health forced him to withdraw. He taught school for a time, and was a clerk in the post office in the Ohio town of Poland when the Civil War broke out.

In June of 1861 young McKinley enlisted as a private in the Ohio 23rd Volunteers, and one of his distinctions was to be the last veteran of the war to occupy the White House. Rutherford B. Hayes, who fought in the same regiment, said: "Young as McKinley was, we soon found that in business and executive ability he was of rare capacity, of unusual and surpassing cleverness for a boy of his age. When battles were fought or a service performed in warlike things, he always took his place." Veterans of the battle of Antietam never forgot McKinley's good sense in filling two wagons with coffee and other supplies and hurrying these refreshments to where the bullets whizzed thickest on that "bloodiest day of the war." President Lincoln made him a major before the war ended.

A career in law and politics absorbed McKinley's interest in the years afterward. In strongly Democratic Stark County, McKinley's victory as the Republican candidate for prosecuting attorney was a tribute to his personal magnetism. At the age of thirty-four, he was elected to Congress where, except for one five-month period, he served continuously for the next twelve years. Always a high-tariff man, McKinley's bill in 1890 baffled friends as well as critics, who wondered why a high duty had been placed on tin plate, which was not being manufactured anywhere in the United States!

The tariff bill of 1890 largely explained McKinley's defeat that year when he ran again for Congress. But there was plenty of political bounce in McKinley. In 1891 he was elected Governor of Ohio and two years later re-elected. His programs to improve Ohio's canals, roads and public institutions brought him national recognition. For all that the inexhaustible Bryan tramped the country in the campaign of 1896, shouting for free silver and an end to the "rule of the rich," the election gave McKinley a comfortable plurality of 601,854 in the popular vote and an electoral victory of 271 to 176.

McKinley took office as President of a country whose citizens were growing increasingly short-tempered over the villainies of Valeriano Weyler y Nicolau, the Spanish Governor of Cuba who herded women and children into concentration camps where they often starved to death. Cuba seethed with revolt, and many Americans—among them Theodore Roosevelt, the Assistant Secretary of the Navy—urged intervention in behalf of the Cuban rebels. McKinley tried to avoid war. Through negotiation he secured the removal of Weyler as Governor of the island and some concessions giving the people a form of self-government.

The war talk lessened. Then, for causes never explained, the American warship *Maine* was blown up in the harbor at Havana. A wave of indignation swept the nation. "Remember the *Maine!*" became the determined cry, calling for an end to Spanish domination in Cuba, and on April 21, 1898, Congress declared war.

The Spanish-American War, lasting 113 days, was one of the strangest conflicts in history. At the battles of San Juan Hill and El Caney, American bluejackets wrested land control of Cuba from Spain, and in June an American fleet under Admiral Sampson cleared the harbor of Santiago of the enemy's warships.

Meanwhile, halfway around the world, another American fleet under Admiral Dewey entered Manila Bay in the Philippines, then a Spanish possession. When the American warships came within range of the enemy, Dewey said coolly to his captain:

"You may fire when you are ready, Gridley."

The battle, beginning in "the misty haze of the tropical dawn," was over by noon. Eight Spanish warships and the shore batteries at Cavite had been destroyed.

Short though the war proved, its impact upon the nation was enormous. At Paris on December 10, 1898, Spain and the United States signed a peace treaty. Cuba was freed. Puerto Rico, the Philippines and Guam became American possessions. When that same year we annexed Hawaii, no one could deny that as the 19th Century approached its close we were becoming a world power. Yet in sending a commission to deal with the Filipinos, President McKinley faced up to this new responsibility with statesmanship, declaring:

"A high and sacred obligation rests upon the Government of the United States to give protection for property and life, civil and religious freedom, and wise, firm and unselfish guidance in the paths of peace and prosperity, to all the people of the Philippine Islands."

Another indication of the new direction in which America was going came in 1900 with the adoption of the "Open Door" policy toward China. The Boxer Rebellion, aimed at driving foreigners from China, resulted in the murder of many missionaries and in attacks upon diplomatic legations at Peking. McKinley sent American troops to restore order, and his "Open Door" notes stressed the wisdom of maintaining an active interest in China trade through peaceful means.

With the election of 1900 Bryan dropped the free silver issue, and with Adlai E. Stevenson of Illinois for a running-mate, stormed the country to attack Republican "imperialism." McKinley, with Theodore Roosevelt for a running-mate, once more let the Democrats do the shouting while he gathered in the votes, this time rolling up a popular plurality of 861,459 and winning the electoral vote 292 to 155.

Big business, delighted with the re-election of McKinley, embarked on a series of mergers to become bigger business, and the notable example was the billion-dollar United States Steel Corporation. With the emergence of the nation as a world power, McKinley took a more moderate position on the tariff, arguing that "the period of exclusiveness is past."

In early September, 1901, McKinley was attending a public reception at the Pan-American Exposition in Buffalo, New York. A young anarchist named Leon Czolgosz approached the President. A handkerchief wrapped around Czolgosz's hand concealed a .32-caliber revolver. Face to face with McKinley, the anarchist fired twice. One bullet struck the President's breastbone and the other entered his abdomen.

"My wife, be careful how you tell her—oh, be careful," pleaded the stricken man.

For eight days McKinley lingered while the country's best surgeons and doctors tried to save his life. Then on September 14, 1901 the country received the grim news—McKinley was dead, the third President to be struck down by an assassin's bullet within a period of thirty-six years. Forty-five days later Czolgosz was electrocuted.

THEODORE ROOSEVELT

"The Rough Rider"

THE SLOPES OF San Juan Hill were covered with guinea grass. Around the blockhouses that the Spaniards held, the red flowers of flame-trees caught the beams of a bright sun. American bluejackets, checking rifles, cartridge belts, bayonets, waited for the command to charge.

A brisk, determined man, riding a horse Western style, rallied the men in his regiment. Big-toothed grin, spectacles perched on his nose, bristling moustache—no one could mistake Theodore Roosevelt who, at the outbreak of the Spanish-American War, had resigned as Assistant Secretary of the Navy to organize his famous Rough Riders.

Around "T. R." clustered the cowboys and Indians from Arizona, New Mexico and Oklahoma, the polo players from Long Island, and the football players from eastern college campuses who had been recruited because they were "young, good shots, and good riders." But this charge they would make on foot—all except their commander, who would lead them up San Juan Hill.

"Are you afraid to stand up when I am on horseback?" Roosevelt asked.

The Rough Riders answered gamely. They'd follow T. R. anywhere! Pistol in hand, Roosevelt waved his boys forward. Spaniards in high-crowned hats waited with rifles raised.

Roosevelt, breaking from a cover of woods, found the men of the Ninth Division lying in his way. "If you don't wish to go forward, let my men pass, please," Roosevelt shouted.

The men of the Ninth sprang into line with the Rough Riders. Richard Harding Davis, watching the bluejackets storm a blockhouse, remembered: "Roosevelt, mounted high on horseback, and charging the rifle-pits at a gallop and quite alone, made you feel that you would like to cheer. He wore on his sombrero a blue polka-dot handkerchief, which, as he advanced, floated out straight behind his head."

San Juan Hill was a bitter, scalding battle. "It was a miracle of self-sacrifice," Davis testified, "a triumph of bulldog courage, which one watched breathless with wonder. The fire of the Spanish riflemen, who still stuck bravely to their posts, doubled and trebled in fierceness, the crests of the hills crackled and burst in amazed roars, and rippled with waves of tiny flame. But the blue line crept steadily up and on, and then, near the top, the broken fragments gathered together with a sudden burst of speed. The Spaniards appeared for a moment outlined against the sky and poised for instant flight, fired a last volley and fled before the swift-moving wave that leaped and sprang up after them."

The victory was of tremendous importance, giving the American troops command of Santiago. And the nation gained a new idol—Colonel Theodore Roosevelt, the Rough Rider—who rode up San Juan Hill.

Like Washington, Jackson, Lincoln, the energetic Roosevelt was a man of history and legend. To the shrewd, conservative political boss,

Mark Hanna, he was "a madman" or "that cowboy." To his enemies he was "a Harvard dude" and a "goo-goo"—political slang for anyone who crusaded for good government. But to the people he became, after San Juan Hill, "Teddy" of the toothsome smile and spectacles.

The Roosevelts were a fine old Dutch family who had come to America in 1644. As landowners and businessmen they had prospered for over two centuries when, on October 27, 1858, Theodore was born in New York City. Affectionately called "Teedie" by his brother and two sisters, he was a frail child who suffered with asthma and weak eyes.

A gymnasium, built on the second floor of the family mansion at 28 East 20th Street, provided Teedie with the punching bag, dumbbells, and horizontal bars to develop his body. "Theodore, you must *make* your body," his father counseled constantly, building in the lad a love for all vigorous pursuits and most of all for life in what he called the "grand but desolate wilds." No one had to worry about stimulating the youngster's mental curiosity—Teedie always had an overdose of that, and maids despaired of cleaning the bedroom where the "Roosevelt Museum of Natural History" included a large assortment of stuffed mice.

The advantages of wealth provided for Teedie good private schools, travel abroad with his family, a Harvard education. At loose ends, he tried studying law but soon wearied of it. He tried writing history, and produced an authoritative and ponderously dull book on *The Naval War of 1812*. He married pretty Alice Lee of Boston, and, completely in character, took time on his European honeymoon to climb the Matterhorn. Two Englishmen recently had made the ascent and their boasting was too much for Teddy, who had to show that the feat wasn't anything special.

Returning to New York, Roosevelt decided that the only career which could truly hold his interest was one in government. It didn't trouble him that members of socially prominent families were supposed to look down their patrician noses at "local politics." In 1881, only twenty-three years of age, he ran for the New York Assembly, won, and to the discomfiture of the city's political bosses embarked with exuberance upon his new life as a "goo-goo." His name was soon in the headlines, for he refused to be hushed up in the case of a judge involved in a scandal. The culprit was impeached.

Re-elected to the Assembly twice, the tragic death of his wife in 1884, coming soon after the death of his beloved mother, dulled the young legislator's enthusiasm as "a member of the governing class." To escape the scenes of this grief, he bought a ranch on the Little Missouri River in North Dakota. Here he sank $50,000 in the cattle business and laughed off the loss. What could be better than a life of "roughing it" —which, to Teddy, meant hunting buffalo, doing the work of a cowboy which was "plumb good sport," and capturing three thieves in the wildest part of the North Dakota Badlands.

"By Godfrey, but this is fun!" sang out Teddy. His best book, *The Winning of the West*, reflected his good time on this adventure.

Yet Teddy had to admit that he was a failure as a rancher. Returning to New York City, he ran for mayor in 1886 and lost. That December he married Edith Kermit Carow, a childhood friend. He turned once more to writing. Then, in 1888, his political future brightened when President Harrison found the ideal spot for a "goo-goo," appointing Teddy a member of the Civil Service Commission.

The Democratic Cleveland reappointed the Republican Roosevelt to the Commission—a tribute to Teddy's energy and effective service— but in 1895 Teddy resigned to become New York City's Police Commissioner. President McKinley, indebted for Teddy's vigorous support in the campaign of 1896, grudgingly named him Assistant Secretary of the Navy. With the outbreak of the Spanish-American War and the organization of the Rough Riders, Teddy's popularity skyrocketed. Within two years his war record carried him to the Governorship of New York and to the Vice-Presidency.

Mark Hanna did not disguise his displeasure at the nomination, grumbling to his friends:

"Don't you realize that there is but one heartbeat between the White House and this madman?"

Six months after Teddy's inauguration as Vice-President an assassin's bullet ended McKinley's life. Teddy came bouncing out of the Adirondacks, where he was on a camping trip, to take the oath of office as twenty-sixth President of the United States. He brought to his tasks, declared Secretary of State John Hay, "the sensibility of a poet and the steel nerve of a Rough Rider." Others had another opinion of Teddy as he switched from a soldier's sombrero to a high hat.

Teddy, as President, was always a state of mind—a man cocksure of himself in making his choice between what constituted "good" or "bad," whether talking about big businesses or little nations. And talk Teddy did constantly, educating the American people to the great problems of the age.

Teddy, the trust-breaker, fighting J. P. Morgan and Company and supporting a whopping fine of $29,000,000 against the Standard Oil Company of Indiana for accepting railroad rebates, was still the Rough Rider to the people.

Teddy, the friend of labor, fighting court interference with the legal right to strike and threatening to use troops to seize the mines if the operators didn't give in to the workers, was still the jaunty colonel galloping over rifle-pits on San Juan Hill.

Teddy, the warrior-peacemaker, chasing Great Britain and Germany out of Venezuela, settling the boundary dispute in Alaska, subduing guerrillas in the Philippines, and bringing envoys of the fighting nations in the Russo-Japanese War to Portsmouth, New Hampshire to sign a treaty, won the Nobel Prize for peace.

The buoyant Teddy easily gained re-election, for the people believed, as a member of the White House staff said, "We woke up every

Stanley Borack

morning wondering what new adventure we were off on when Roosevelt was President." Among his greatest achievements was the construction of the Panama Canal, though to secure the land that would link the two oceans his methods were high-handed. Strictly speaking, Teddy did not instigate a revolt in Colombia, but within three days after the revolution took place, he recognized the Republic of Panama and American naval vessels discouraged Colombian troops from fighting.

"I took Panama without consulting the Cabinet," Teddy confessed. And he admitted: "I took the Isthmus, started the canal, and then left Congress—not to debate the canal, but to debate me." With a sudden grin, he added: "But while the debate goes on, the canal does too."

Teddy selected William Howard Taft as his successor in the White House. But Teddy was soon back in the headlines as the restless little man took his twenty-two-year-old son Kermit and the gold-mounted rabbit's foot that the prize fighter, John L. Sullivan, had given him and plunged into Darkest Africa on a big-game hunt. Seventeen lions were among the five hundred animals and birds that the two Roosevelts bagged. And he was "delighted"—favorite Roosevelt word—to find what to do with ex-Presidents: "They can be used to scare rhinos away."

In June, 1910, when Teddy returned to New York, he received a rousing welcome. Soon he was deep in politics, and, characteristically, he stirred up a hornets' nest. Private property, insisted Teddy, was held subject "to the general right of the community to regulate its use to whatever degree the public welfare may require it." President Taft and conservative Republican leaders threw up their hands. This fellow was an outright socialist!

Merrily, Teddy went his own way. When the election of 1912 approached, he bolted the Republican Party and formed the Progressive Party. "I feel as fit as a bull moose," he announced gaily, and as the "Bull Moose" candidate he pulled more votes than Taft, but so badly split the Republicans that the Democratic candidate won easily.

158

Teddy had held his last public office. His impact upon the country still endures. He was a militant spokesman for the conservation of the nation's natural resources. His policy to "Speak softly and carry a big stick" found him an aggressive advocate of a large army and navy. Under his administrations the Federal Meat-Inspection Act and the Pure Food Law of 1906 were typical of the progressive legislation that made Teddy a respected "goo-goo."

In 1914 Teddy was back in the headlines, this time joining an expedition to explore the River of Doubt deep in the Brazilian jungles. Now in his mid-fifties, Teddy wanted a "last chance to be a boy," and it almost cost him his life. Savage piranha fish bit off part of the foot of a colonel, four men died, another lost his mind and killed a comrade, and for a time the party subsisted on monkeys. Teddy, suffering an abscess, ran a fever of 105° and, believing he had become a burden to the others, pleaded to be left in the jungles. But the old bounce saved him, and he was joyously welcomed home.

In 1916 the Progressive Party wanted to run Teddy for President, but he knew the Bull Moose movement was played out and declined. He never forgave President Wilson for refusing to allow him, during World War I, to organize and lead another regiment like his beloved Rough Riders. In 1916 he wrote out for an editor the "things that America needs:

"1. That every molly-coddle, professional pacifist, and man who is 'too proud to fight' when the nation's quarrel is just, should be exiled to those out of the way parts . . . where the spirit of manliness has not yet penetrated.

"2. That every decent young man should have a family, a job, and military training which will enable him to help keep this country out of war by making it dangerous for any ruthless military people to attack us.

"3. That every youngster may have a good and wise mother; and every good woman a child for her arms.

"4. That we may all of us become an efficient, patriotic, and nobly proud people—too proud either to inflict wrong or to endure it."

Ill health began to plague Teddy in 1918, and the death of his son Quentin became a deep, lingering grief. Americans loved him deeply, and a boom started to make him the Republican presidential nominee in 1920. On January 6, 1919, death came in his sleep at his home, Sagamore Hill, in Oyster Bay, New York.

Cowboy, historian, police commissioner, naval secretary, Rough Rider, Governor, Vice-President, President, peacemaker, hunter and explorer—for frail little Teedie life had turned out to be quite "bully."

WILLIAM HOWARD TAFT

"Big Bill"

ONLY ONCE in American history have the two highest offices in the country—President of the United States and Chief Justice of the Supreme Court—been held by the same man. He was smiling, affable William Howard Taft, whom friends called "Big Bill."

The ponderous Taft, who stood six-feet-two and weighed over three hundred pounds, also came close to being our unhappiest President. Once he described the White House as "the lonesomest place in the world." Even the fact that he was the first President to take up golf as a hobby, to drive around Washington in an electric car, or to receive $75,000 a year for his services could not compensate for the four bitter years he experienced.

Yet Taft could not deny that he was warned against becoming President. His mother insisted that the White House was no place for her good-humored son. "His is a judicial mind and he loves the law," declared Mrs. Taft in the mother-knows-best tradition. After all, from that fifteenth day of September, 1857, when Bill Taft was born in Cincinnati, Ohio, he had grown up in an atmosphere where the decent life consisted of practicing law and voting Republican. His father, Alphonso Taft, had served in Grant's Cabinet as Secretary of War and Attorney General and later as United States Minister to Austria and Russia.

Except for a brief fling as a newspaper reporter, everything in Bill Taft's early career found him following faithfully in the footsteps of a distinguished father. He attended the public schools in Cincinnati, and then went to Yale, his father's university, where despite occasional fits of laziness Big Bill graduated second in his class. As assistant prosecutor for Ohio's Hamilton County, and then as assistant solicitor, he compiled creditable records.

Obviously Papa's prominence in Republican politics did not handicap young Taft, who advanced steadily as a judge of the Ohio Superior Court, as Solicitor General of the United States and then as a judge of the Federal Court of Appeals by appointment of President Harrison. If as a Federal judge Taft's opinions tended to restrict the labor movement, his attitudes scarcely made him unattractive to the conservative wing of his party. Mama Taft was delighted with Big Bill's success as a judge, but his wife, the former Edith Herron, wanted her husband to seek greater ambitions. Caught in this tug of wills between two strong-minded women, Taft tried to please both, which was impossible.

In 1901, by appointment of President McKinley, Taft became the first civil governor of the Philippine Islands. He called the Filipinos "my little brown brothers" and was devoted to their interests. New systems of courts, land records, sanitary regulations and schools were established as Taft made his administration of the Philippines a model of enlightened colonial government. He allowed no color line to be drawn in dealing with his brown brothers and cracked down on army officers who wanted to substitute force for reason and fair play in dealing with the Filipinos. Teddy Roosevelt twice offered Taft a place on the Supreme Court, which he dearly coveted, and twice Taft declined the appointment. His first duty was to the Filipinos.

In 1904 Teddy recalled Taft to Washington to become Secretary of War. As Teddy's principal "trouble-shooter," Taft supervised construction of the Panama Canal and worked out a system of government in the Canal Zone. Teddy called Taft "the most lovable personality" he ever had known, personally pushed him into the presidential nomination of 1908, and saw him win easily over Bryan with a popular plurality of 1,269,900 and an electoral majority of 321 to 162.

The four years that Taft occupied the White House found America coming together like a gangling boy who, all at once, reaches his full growth and loses his awkwardness. The admission of Arizona and New Mexico to the Union brought the number of states to forty-eight. With Robert E. Peary going to the North Pole and Roald Amundsen traveling to the South Pole, people began visualizing a world with a top and bottom. Henry Ford began producing his Model T or "Tin Lizzie" on a mass-production basis and by 1913 was supplying a restless America with almost a thousand automobiles a day. Three years earlier Glenn H. Curtis fascinated the public imagination by flying an airplane from Albany to New York City in two hours and fifty-one minutes.

In short, America had entered an age of the aggressive, imaginative showman, such as Teddy Roosevelt had been and Taft could never be. Yet slow, cautious, plodding though our twenty-seventh President was, his enemies underestimated his great wisdom and unfailing honesty. No one could get jolly Big Bill Taft to smoke or take a drink—he was set in his ways—but he was set also in his principles. Teddy, of course, always shouted that he was on God's side, fighting against the devil. Taft was quieter, and, surprisingly, sometimes more effective.

Teddy won renown as the great "trust-buster," but Taft actually did more trust-busting in four years in office than Teddy did in seven.

Teddy, with his policy of speaking softly and carrying a big stick, won renown for vitalizing America's place in world affairs, but Taft gave to "dollar diplomacy" the obligation of using trade and commerce to increase American prestige abroad rather than using diplomacy to expand commerce. A lover of peace, he avoided intervention with a Mexico in revolution, although in the end he simply left a situation for another President to solve.

The establishment of the Department of Labor and the Federal Children's Bureau, the granting of full territorial government for Alaska, and the creation of the Parcel Post and Postal Savings were other achievements of Taft's Administration. A Commerce Court was organized and the powers of the Interstate Commerce Commission expanded. The Sixteenth Amendment, authorizing a Federal income tax, and the Seventeenth Amendment, providing for the popular election of United States Senators became part of our basic law.

For showmanship Taft substituted faithful service. It was not enough. Teddy, full of vigor as the election of 1912 approached and scandalizing conservative Republicans with the social reforms he advocated, now called Taft "useless to the American people." With the Bull Moosers splitting the Republicans wide open, the electoral vote in 1912 was what everyone expected: Taft, 8; Roosevelt, 88; Woodrow Wilson, 435.

Mother Taft had been right. The White House was no place for her Bill. With good humor, Taft left Washington to become a professor of law at Yale and later President of the American Bar Association. In 1921 came his appointment as Chief Justice of the Supreme Court, and for the next eight years he began every day exuberantly at five-fifteen in the morning. Failing health forced him to resign only a little more than a month before his death on March 8, 1930. In large part the story of his life was made in a comment during his years as Chief Justice:

"I don't remember that I was ever President!"

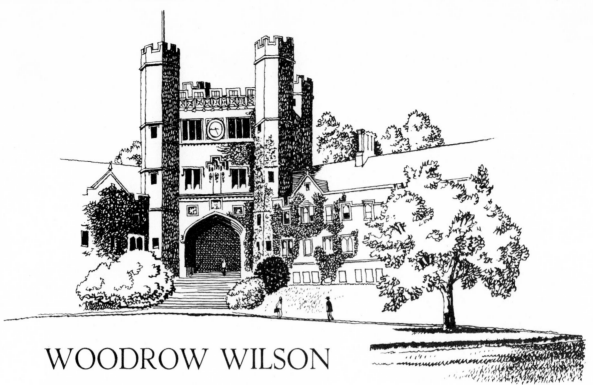

WOODROW WILSON
"A World Safe for Democracy"

T HERE IS such a thing as a man being too proud to fight." Thus
spoke Woodrow Wilson, twenty-eighth President of the United
States, in May, 1915 as he tried to avoid American involvement in a
European war.

"The world must be made safe for democracy. Its peace must be
planted upon the tested foundations of political liberty." Wilson spoke
solemnly on a day in 1917, when the country entered World War I.

"There will come sometime…another struggle in which, not a few
hundred thousand fine men from America will have to die, but many
millions…to accomplish the final freedom of the peoples of the world."
Wilson, near the end of life, spoke now to save the League of Nations, his
dream of settling disputes through international fellowship.

Not since Thomas Jefferson had any man occupied the White House
who could equal Wilson's accomplishments as a scholar of government.

Not since Abraham Lincoln had any President surpassed Wilson in the ability to move people to extremes of frantic devotion and explosive hatred. Not even the effervescent Teddy Roosevelt could outmatch the aloof Wilson in his confidence that he knew what was "good" and "bad" for the country. He stood apart from every chief executive except Lincoln who also was President and prophet in one.

Thomas Woodrow Wilson, born at Staunton, Virginia on December 28, 1856, inherited the disrupted life that the Civil War brought to many children. Not until the age of nine was he able to start school and not until eleven was he able to read with ease. Pitifully weak eyes also contributed to his slow progress and forced him to drop out of Davidson College before he completed his freshman year. But there was Scotch-Irish tenacity in young Wilson, a will to learn that he absorbed from his father, a devout Presbyterian clergyman and teacher.

So two years later, in 1875, his health restored, Wilson entered Princeton University. Again he experienced a difficult freshman year and carried home a poor scholastic record. But the determined young man kept plugging, and when he graduated stood thirty-eighth in a class of 106. A course at the law school of the University of Virginia followed, and then Wilson went to Atlanta, Georgia and hopefully hung up his shingle as a young lawyer.

Wilson attracted few clients. With time hanging heavily, an interest in history and politics took hold of him, and he decided to close his law office. As a graduate student at Johns Hopkins University, he prepared for a new career as a college professor.

Wilson had found his niche. Books on *Congressional Government* and *The State* established his reputation as a profound student of politics and government. He taught for a time at Bryn Mawr College, but felt uncomfortable in a girls' school. Later as a professor at Wesleyan University and Princeton, his fame as a scholar grew. Almost yearly he turned down offers to become a college president.

Yet, in Macaulay's phrase, Wilson was no book in breeches. At Wesleyan he coached the football team. He was an inveterate composer of humorous limericks and liked a good vaudeville show. Usually students called him the best lecturer they knew—tough in his standards, but capable of putting a point across so that it stuck in their minds. In 1902 the trustees of Princeton, where the president always had been a clergyman, voted to make an exception by offering the position to Wilson.

He accepted, but on a condition. He didn't believe in a university that was a place where "youngsters" were doing "tasks." A university, he said, should be a place "where there are men thinking."

In this spirit, Wilson as President of Princeton had his triumphs and headaches. His effort to reform Princeton eating-clubs, which resembled fraternities, brought angry alumni storming back in protest. They didn't care if Wilson did think the eating-clubs were undemocratic; they wanted the clubs left alone. In the public mind, rightly or wrongly, Wilson was identified with fighting against snobbery. His popularity bounded upward, and was the principal reason why, one day in 1910, he was summoned from a golf game to take a surprising phone call.

How would Wilson like to be Governor of New Jersey, asked the voice at the other end of the connection. In a then solidly Republican state, Democratic bosses were ecstatic at their inspiration to nominate a highly respected college president who would be too dumb to interfere with the operations of machine politics. Wilson easily won the election and kicked out the political bosses.

But while the bosses sulked, the people of New Jersey rejoiced to have their government run well. Passage of a primary election law, a corrupt practices act, a public utilities and an employers' liability act, a law permitting reform in municipal government and several school reforms established Wilson as the greatest "goo-goo" fighting for good government in the country. When he wanted something done, and legislators balked, he carried his cause to the people.

With the Republicans split in 1912 between Taft and Roosevelt factions, the Democrats realized when they gathered for their national convention in Baltimore that whomever they nominated was certain to win. Old progressives like William Jennings Bryan had no taste for the leading candidate, "Champ" Clark of Missouri, who was suspected of being in cahoots with the bosses of Tammany Hall. On the thirteenth ballot Bryan swung his support to Wilson, beginning a slow, dogged shift that dragged on until the forty-eighth ballot before Wilson was nominated.

Wisely, Wilson held aloof from the Taft vs. Roosevelt bickering, and his temperate statements made him more popular with the public. The election found him carrying the electoral vote in all but eight states, though the popular tally gave a plurality to the two Republican candidates: Wilson, 6,286,214; Roosevelt, 4,216,020; Taft, 3,482,922.

The real job of a government, declared Wilson in his inaugural address, was to serve "humanity," and in the record of his first administration he did not forsake "all forward-looking men" upon whom he called to help him. A tariff bill lowered duties, a graduated income tax exempted earnings up to $3,000 a year, the Federal Reserve Act stood as a monument to statesmanship in currency and banking legislation, the Federal Trade Commission investigated and ended many unfair trade practices, and a new Pure Food Law increased its protection to consumers. Though he kept Congress in session longer than any President in history, even legislators admitted that he was probably the country's most constructive chief executive since George Washington.

In foreign affairs, Wilson scrapped the doctrine of "dollar diplomacy." Inheriting from Taft an open break with a revolutionary Mexican Government, he established a new principle in American history by permitting the ABC powers (Argentina, Brazil and Chile) to arbitrate the dispute in an international conference. But a new revolution, led by Francisco Villa, brought Wilson to sterner measures when this bandit chief killed fifteen Americans in a raid on Columbus, New Mexico. Troops under General John J. Pershing marched into Mexico and put a stop to Villa's banditry. Since Pershing once had commanded Negro troops, he became an American idol as "Black Jack." Events in Europe, beginning in 1914, soon would draw both President Wilson and "Black Jack" Pershing toward a fame neither wanted.

Behind these tragic events were three words, *Drang nach Osten*, meaning "Push toward the East." In Austria, for example, *Drang nach Osten* meant finding an excuse for overrunning the little countries of Serbia and Montenegro to secure a port on the Adriatic Sea. Austria expected to gain her goal with a quick little war, but instead she and her allies (Germany, Turkey and Bulgaria) became locked in a death struggle with such powers as Britain, France, Belgium and Russia.

Wilson tried to remain neutral as World War I swept over Europe. Women gathered before the White House and sang, "I Didn't Raise My Boy to Be a Soldier." Running for re-election against a powerful Republican candidate, Chief Justice Charles Evans Hughes, Wilson promised the American people: "I know that you are depending upon me to keep this nation out of war. So far I have done so and I pledge you my word that, God helping me, I will—if it is possible." Largely because of the slogan, "He kept us out of war," Wilson defeated Hughes by the close electoral vote of 277 to 254.

Actually the American people scarcely had been neutral in spirit. American farms and factories were pouring out the supplies on which Britain and other Allied Powers depended. In retaliation, German submarines launched a concentrated attack on American shipping, which inflamed American tempers to the breaking point. On Good Friday, 1917, we declared war on Germany. We were waging, we cried, "a war to end war," a war "to make the world safe for democracy."

And fight we did, with a will and an idealism never before known in history. Factories and shipyards worked day and night. We bought

Liberty Bonds and paid ever-increasing taxes. We "economized" and accepted "meatless days" so that food could be sent to our soldiers and friends overseas. Children collected balls of tinfoil needed in war materials and wives, mothers and sisters knitted millions of miles of woolen socks for doughboy husbands, sons and sweethearts.

Gaily singing, "We won't be back till it's over, over there," thousands of Americans sailed to bloody battles whose very names left a chill in American hearts—Belleau Woods, where 6,000 out of 8,000 American marines perished, and Château-Thierry, where a costly American counter-attack saved Paris. Later came the torture of Saint-Mihiel, the desperate, sunless struggle in the Argonne Forest, before the war ended on November 11, 1918 and Johnny could march home, as the song promised, to K-k-k-katie waiting at the k-k-k-kitchen door.

In a brilliant speech President Wilson already had enumerated the famous "Fourteen Points" on which he believed the peace settlement must be based. No private international diplomacy, freedom of the seas, limitation of armaments, open-minded adjustment of colonial claims—in such terms of statesmanlike fairness Wilson spelled out his plan. The last of his points contained his dream that the conflict truly would become a war to end war and asked for "a general association of nations formed under specific covenants to guarantee political independence and territorial integrity to all countries."

A hero's reception awaited Wilson when he reached Paris for the Peace Conference. Though forced to give in on many minor points, on his great dream—the establishment of the League of Nations—he won his way through the sheer power of his prestige with the people of the world.

In 1919 America had not yet caught up to a changing world. The year before the establishment of the first airmail route and the year following the beginning of commercial radio broadcasting indicated the increased speed with which men and ideas were soon to travel. But many did not see the future with Wilson's clear, brilliant mind. They still relied on two oceans to protect America from future foreign entanglements, and these "isolationists" in Congress prevented our membership in the League of Nations by refusing to give the two-thirds majority necessary for the ratification of any treaty.

Wilson acted in character—he went directly to the people. Doctors warned him that his health was failing, but their advice to rest only spurred his determination to attempt a speaking tour in the Middle and Far West. On September 25, 1919, he spoke at Pueblo, Colorado, and that night sped eastward on a train toward Wichita, Kansas. Then came bleak news—the President had collapsed. He returned to Washington, an invalid and desperately sick man.

Even on a sickbed, Wilson would not give up the fight. He insisted that his party make ratification of the League of Nations the main issue in the campaign of 1920. The Republicans, opposing the League, won an easy victory with Warren G. Harding as their presidential candidate.

Calm and dignified, Wilson left the White House, insisting that time would prove him right. The United States could no longer hide behind its oceans. It must lend its support and power to a community of nations wherein some better method than war could be employed to settle disputes. On February 3, 1924 he died in his home in Washington and was buried in the National Cathedral. Like a clarion call, many remembered that Good Friday in 1917 when, asking Congress for a declaration of war, Wilson had spoken his faith as a great American:

"...we shall fight for the things which we have always carried nearest our hearts—for democracy for the right of those who submit to authority to have a voice in their own Government, for the rights and liberties of small nations, for a universal domination of right by such a concert of free people as shall bring peace and safety to all nations and make the world itself at last free."

Only the man had died. His dream still lived.

WARREN G. HARDING

"The Man from Main Street"

HENRY M. DAUGHERTY, the Ohio political boss who discovered in young Warren G. Harding the qualities of a natural vote-getter, once said: "I found him sunning himself, like a turtle on a log, and I pushed him into the water." For the twenty-ninth President of the United States there came a day when he had reason to wonder if Mr. Daugherty had done him any great favor. Oil and water do not mix, and therein rested Harding's trouble.

The boy who, on November 2, 1865, was born on a farm near Blooming Grove, Ohio, never dreamed of being President. His father, a farmer who later became a doctor, was descended from an English family that had landed at Plymouth in 1620, but Warren Gamaliel Harding wasn't likely to mention that fact to the crowd down on Main Street. What did they care? And Harding, boy and man, always belonged to the Main Street of small towns. He was a good-natured fellow, easy-going, no fancy

174

airs, happy to toot a horn in the band at Caledonia High and content to grin his way through four pleasant years at Ohio Central College.

In 1882, when his father moved to the little town of Marion, Harding secured his first job as a typesetter on the weekly *Democratic Mirror*. His wages, a dollar a week, weren't magnificent, but then a chap had to start somewhere. And in 1884 they stopped suddenly, as he might have expected, when he too warmly supported James G. Blaine, the Republican candidate for President.

But Warren Harding laughed. The world had worse troubles. With a friend he raised $300 and bought the *Marion Star*, another weekly. The paper's circulation was small, but again, why fret? Marion was going to grow as a town. The *Star* would grow with it. And Warren Harding likewise grew—handsome and big-framed with a wonderful speaking voice and an engaging smile. In 1891 the *Star* carried a real news story. At twenty-six he was marrying Florence De Wolfe Kling, daughter of the town's leading banker. Warren Harding, accepting her wealth and social influence in stride, called her "the Duchess."

Everybody liked Harding. No one who worked for him was ever fired. He never said "no" to a panhandler. He joined everything, chewed tobacco, knew the batting averages of the baseball greats, took a drink, enjoyed poker or golf or just chinning on a street corner. He was everybody's friend. In the State Senate he served two terms, and his affability wasn't missed by Mr. Daugherty, who "pushed him into the water."

What this meant, specifically, was one term as Lieutenant Governor of Ohio, an unsuccessful bid for the Governorship, then election in 1914 to the United States Senate, where Harding was still serving when the Republicans met to nominate a national ticket in 1920 that would bury the League of Nations along with James Cox and Franklin D. Roosevelt, the Democratic candidates.

The Republicans, convening in Chicago, were soon hopelessly deadlocked among too many strong candidates. But Henry M. Daugherty, battlewise in politics, had expected this to happen. He waited until the front-runners had worn nerves edgy, then quietly called a group of senators to "a smoke-filled room" in the early hours of the morning and maneuvered the nomination that Harding didn't want. With the political reaction that inevitably dominates a country after a war, it was almost impossible for him to lose the election. His campaign stretched no further than the front porch of his home in Marion, Ohio. The time had come, he said, for "America first" and a "return to normalcy." Enough Americans agreed to send him into the White House on a landslide vote.

Not since Grant had Washington encountered a President less qualified for the job. By negotiating separate peace treaties with Germany, Hungary and Austria the Harding Administration found a way of scrapping the League of Nations and though it was agreed the United States should join the World Court, so many limitations were imposed that the court was virtually powerless. A "return to normalcy," by Harding's actions, meant high tariffs, reduction of taxes for those in higher income brackets, and a government that protected business from the abuses of labor. It also seemed a good idea to hunt down "radicals," whenever the Department of Justice could find them.

Still, Harding, were it not for his friends, might have lived out an unruffled term in the White House. The nation responded with deep emotion in 1921 to the burial of the Unknown Soldier in Arlington National Cemetery, and to the dedication a year later of the magnificent Lincoln Memorial in Washington. A Disarmament Conference in Washington found the countries of the world moving toward a lasting peace—at least on paper. The people, absorbed by their new crystal set radios, even heard the voice of the President of the United States in the earphones strapped to their heads. To divert other Americans, Babe Ruth slapped out home runs for the New York Yankees, a revived Ku Klux Klan was back in its bedsheets spreading hatred for Jews, Negroes, Catholics, and foreigners in general, and a new magazine called *Time* appeared.

Stanley Gersh

On March 4, 1923, however, a badly troubled President accepted the resignation of Albert B. Fall, his Secretary of the Interior. A story of scandal in government, such as Grant had suffered by trusting his friends with a faith they ill repaid, soon was in the open. Involved were oil reserves belonging to the Navy and known as Teapot Dome and Elk Hills that, for a bribe, Secretary Fall had leased to private interests. Fall ultimately went to jail, but the accusations of malpractice went further, involving Edwin Denby, the Secretary of the Navy, and agents of the Department of Justice and the Veterans' Bureau.

Harding was staggered by the disclosures. Growlish demands that he should be impeached made the unhappy man wish he were back on Main Street, where he belonged. That June he set off on a speechmaking tour with his family and traveled as far as Alaska. The President was reported suffering with ptomaine poisoning and returned to San Francisco, haggard and exhausted. Pneumonia followed; then suddenly on August 2, he died. The scandals and vilifications of past weeks seemed instantly forgotten. People lined the route of his funeral train. An American President was dead. His nation sorrowed for him.

CALVIN COOLIDGE

"The business of America is business"

C ALVIN could get more sap out of a maple tree than any other boy
around here."

The proud man speaking was the father of John Calvin Coolidge, thirtieth President of the United States, who was born in the little Vermont village of Plymouth Notch on July 4, 1872. Descended from a family that had come to Vermont sometime around 1630, young Calvin —the lad soon dropped the John—was as typical a product of New England as baked beans, brown bread and the first Thanksgiving.

Not even one of the early Adamses could cling more zealously than Calvin Coolidge to the belief that hard work, common sense, and the ability to spend less than you earned were the secrets to a happy life. Upon these three principles Calvin Coolidge shaped his career from those boyhood years when he worked in the fields and clerked in his father's store until, at Harding's death, he moved into the White House.

No one could ever deny that the formula had not worked wonderfully for Calvin Coolidge. As a student at Black River Academy, St. Johnsbury Academy and Amherst College he had excelled through diligent effort. As a lawyer afterward in Northampton, Massachusetts he had stuck out the first few lean and hungry years to become a respected and prosperous member of his profession. And as a politician, he probably held more offices than any other President.

Coolidge's progress in politics began in 1898 with his election to the Northampton city council. A year later he was city solicitor. In 1906, now the best Republican campaign manager in Hampshire County, he was sent to the Massachusetts House of Representatives. Two terms as mayor of Northampton followed, then four years as a state senator. In 1915 he was elected Lieutenant Governor and three years later stepped into the Governorship.

Boston policemen in 1919, determined to form a union within the American Federation of Labor, went on strike. Charging that policemen did not possess the right to strike, the city's police commissioner discharged nineteen leaders of the union movement. Other policemen walked out, saying they would stay out until those nineteen jobs were restored. Citizens of Boston shivered at the threat to their security, city units of the militia were called on duty, then Governor Coolidge ordered out the entire State Guard.

"There is no right to strike against the public safety by anybody, anywhere, any time," he declared.

Overnight, by a single act, Calvin Coolidge became a national celebrity. Congratulations came to him from President Wilson. In the public mind he typified that calm strength so necessary to a sound leader, and as this conviction grew it one day gave the country a ringing slogan: "Keep cool with Coolidge." The Republican convention that nominated the virtually unknown Harding added Coolidge as his running-mate to bolster the popular appeal of the ticket.

As Vice-President, Coolidge presided over the Senate and otherwise minded his business. Even then he was acquiring a mild fame as "Silent Cal," the frugal New Englander who seemed to hate wasting words as much as needlessly spending a dollar. He was in Northampton, visiting his father, when news of Harding's death reached him. At two in the morning of August 3, 1923 he awakened his father, who was a justice of the peace, and took the oath of office.

Little more than a year of Harding's term remained, but no one doubted that conservative Republicans intended to renominate in 1924 a sound candidate who, like Coolidge, declared: "The business of America is business." Nor was there any doubt that he would be re-elected at a time when the country was considered more prosperous than it ever had been. The profound changes that were taking place in America and in the world—changes illustrated by army fliers completing the first flight around the world in 1924, and by Lindbergh's solo nonstop flight from New York to Paris and the inauguration of transatlantic radio telephone service in 1927—were only vaguely grasped. In the carefree 1920's when a congressman danced the Charleston on Capitol grounds and talking motion pictures were a new craze, no one was worrying much about the future.

To a slap-happy America there was a comforting sense of security in newspaper pictures of Coolidge greeting a delegation of Sioux Indians on the White House lawn. And businessmen, with the stock market at an all time high, nodded approval when Coolidge remarked that there were only two ways in which a person could be self-respecting: "To spend less than you make, and to make more than you spend." The dream of America was that its good times would endure forever.

There were murmurings, ominous and unhappy, that were ignored. When twice Coolidge vetoed bills intended to help hard-pressed farmers by buying their surplus crops to sell abroad, few tried to probe deeply into what happened to a once predominantly agricultural country when it became industrialized. A few old followers of that Republican-turned-socialist, Teddy Roosevelt, might grumble at the veto of a bill intended to turn Muscle Shoals over to the Government as an electric power project, but, said the vast majority, all business, including public utilities, belonged in the hands of private investors. Certainly no isolationist objected when Coolidge insisted that the nations we had helped in the World War should pay back the money they had borrowed. If they didn't have the money, let them work hard and make it.

A high tariff, restriction on immigration, reduced taxes for those making big salaries—in essence, these were the sum of Coolidge's domestic policies. In foreign affairs, never an internationally-minded man, the President was fortunate in his selection of Dwight W. Morrow as Ambassador to Mexico, for relations with our southern neighbors were placed on a completely happy basis, and with the signing of the Kellogg-Briand Pact at Paris in 1928 practically all the civilized nations of the world agreed to outlaw war.

On an August day the year before, when the boom was growing to re-run Coolidge for the Presidency, he handed newspapermen a brief note. It read:

"I do not choose to run for President in nineteen twenty-eight."

Nor did he. He listened smilingly as his successor, President Herbert Hoover, assured the people in his acceptance speech, "the poorhouse is vanishing from among us," and made his plans to return to Northampton and buy a home. Here he lived until his death of a heart attack on January 5, 1933, writing a column for newspapers and serving as head of the Advisory Council of the National Economy League, as a trustee of Amherst College, and as a member of the board of directors of the New York Life Insurance Company. Men out of work, selling apples on corners as the country was gripped in its worst depression, read of his death and said:

"Coolidge, he was smart. He knew when to quit."

HERBERT HOOVER

"World Humanitarian"

GERMAN TROOPS, overrunning Belgium in 1914, threw Europe into chaos. Among the 200,000 Americans overseas at the time, who were caught in the cross-current of war with reservations for passage home suddenly canceled, was a world-famous engineer named Herbert Hoover. A man who had risen from scrimpy circumstances to become a multimillionaire, Hoover was respected for his ability to get things done. Even our Ambassador in London appealed to Hoover to help stranded Americans return home by securing loans and passages.

And Hoover did. But he saw another responsibility to discharge — one that would write his name in history and in the hearts of people as a great humanitarian. With the German invasion, the Government of Belgium had fled and the citizens of this stricken little country faced starvation. Hoover could not put their pitiful situation out of his mind. Somehow they should — they must — be fed.

Beginning in October, 1914, Hoover threw the full resources of his heart and mind into this stupendous effort. He traveled across Belgium, France, Great Britain and the United States, gathering food to distribute to the starving and the destitute. How many times he risked passing through the German submarine blockade became a fascinating speculation.

On at least sixty voyages, devoted to but one purpose, he saw the need beyond the personal danger. In time, even the warring nations accepted his mission as one that must be placed above man's passions. Here was a man who handled a billion dollars, and could tell where every penny had gone. Here was a man who served God.

When, in April of 1917, we entered the war, President Wilson appointed Herbert Hoover head of the United States Food Administration Bureau. Soon he accomplished what no other American of his age had done—he made his name a word in the people's language. To "Hooverize" meant to sacrifice willingly that others might eat. Not to cut down on the use of sugar, flour and meat—not to "Hooverize" because it was the decent thing to do though no law said you must—was to be something less than a self-respecting American.

A man and a symbol, a dynamo of human energy and an inspiration —this was Herbert Hoover during World War I, a man whose conscience was a dinner guest in almost every home, every restaurant across America. When the war ended, others cheered and tried to forget the sad, bloody ordeal, but Hoover was back to Europe. Millions of people among both our allies and former enemies remained to be fed. In succeeding months the name of Herbert Hoover became a household word, a synonym for humanity and brotherhood, in France, Germany, Belgium, Poland, Austria, Hungary.

An Iowa farm boy, born near the little town of West Branch on August 10, 1874, even before the war Hoover had roamed the world as though it were hitched to his existence like the yard next door. By the age of ten both of his Quaker parents had died and the orphaned boy was raised by sympathetic uncles, first in Iowa and then in Oregon. He picked up an education in public schools wherever he happened to be. Serving as an office boy in his uncle's real estate agency, Hoover became interested in engineering and this ambition made him a member of the first class to graduate from Leland Stanford University.

Hoover's first job was in the engineering office of Louis Janin in San Francisco. Starting as a clerk, he quickly attracted Janin's interest as a young man with a future. At the age of twenty-three Hoover found himself bound for Australia to take charge of a gold mine.

That was the beginning. Next he was bound for the Orient with a new bride and a new position as chief engineer for the Chinese Imperial Bureau of Mines. In Tientsin when the Boxer Rebellion occurred, Hoover built the defense wall around the foreign concession that saved the necks of his white-skinned comrades. In later years, in business for himself with offices as widely separated as San Francisco and London and with as many as 175,000 people working for him, Hoover was likely to pop up anywhere—in Nicaragua or Mexico, Alaska or South Africa, Belgium or Borneo, Burma or Russia. The dust of five continents was shaken from his wardrobe.

One of the world's leading engineers, one of the world's greatest humanitarians, that was Hoover's completely unpolitical record when President Wilson appointed him to a war job. Both Democrats and Republicans wanted to claim him, now that he was a public figure, and both spoke of him as a possible presidential candidate in 1920. In the Cabinets of Harding and Coolidge his prestige grew as a capable Secretary of Commerce.

When Coolidge "did not choose to run," Hoover became the logical Republican candidate. Al Smith, the boy from the sidewalks of New York who had risen to become Governor and to make the brown derby he wore famous, was named his Democratic opponent. Shameful elements of bigotry in a predominantly Protestant country doubtless hurt the candidacy of Smith, who was Roman Catholic. The chap who at a Boston rally cried, "It ain't Irish Catholics I hate, but just them *Roman Catholics*" revealed the silly, empty-headed extremes to which such prejudice could go.

And likely what damaged Smith's chances of victory even more was an era of prosperity, when "a chicken in every pot and a car in every garage" had become an accepted way of life. Carrying all but eight states in 1928, Hoover became the thirty-first President in one of the most overwhelming victories in American political history.

The nation settled back to four more fat, pleasant years. Then on October 29, 1929 came the crash. In that single day 16,000,000 shares were traded on the Stock Market at an average loss of forty points a share! Dazed, panic-stricken men stood on the sidewalk of Wall Street.

Sincerely, Hoover spoke the faith of his heart. Business, he insisted, was fundamentally sound. Stand firm, he beseeched America—"prosperity is just around the corner." But as weeks passed the panic grew, and suddenly it was widespread. People stopped buying. Factories shut down. Farmers saw their homes swept away by mortgage foreclosures. Hunger drove people into breadlines, demanding that the Government feed them. Veterans of World War I marched on Washington, building shacks out of scrap lumber and declaring that here they would stay until the Government paid their bonuses—in full, in cash. At the President's order, the shacks were burned and Federal troops dispersed the veterans.

An unhappy, bewildered nation struck back with angry words. Somebody was to blame for the hunger, the fear. The President—Hoover—that apple-cheeked stooge of the rich—he was at fault. In a situation that was difficult to understand because there was no complete body of experience by which to judge the problem, men didn't want an appeal to reason. They wanted relief.

With courage, Hoover tried to meet the emergencies of a deepening depression. He did his best, as a trained businessman who thought in the terms of sound economic principles as he had lived them all his life. When nations defaulted on war debts they couldn't pay, he declared a holiday, or moratorium, on such debts. When Great Britain went off the gold standard, leading thirty other nations to follow that course, we held firm to the gold standard, depending on the wisdom of the past. The Reconstruction Finance Corporation was established to loan Federal money to businesses and banks to keep them from closing and the Federal Home Loan made loans through financial institutions to halt the avalanche of mortgage foreclosures.

"Too little and too late," the Democrats cried at whatever Hoover attempted as the election of 1932 approached. Ten million men were out of work, and those selling apples on street corners scarcely earned a decent living. With the national temper heated to the boiling point, it was no surprise when the Democratic candidate, Franklin D. Roosevelt, won by an electoral vote of 427 to 59. With six months still to serve as President, Hoover invited Roosevelt to the White House to join in some action or statement that might revive the nation's confidence. Mr. Roosevelt would not commit himself on whether he favored huge governmental loans for relief at the expense of an unbalanced budget. Banks closing in Michigan began a new wave of pessimism and despair that carried the depression to its lowest level.

Hoover devoted the next few years to enjoying the California sunshine in his home at Palo Alto, to writing and collecting books about World War I that he gave to Stanford University, and to attacking what he believed were the radical and unwise policies of Roosevelt. Yet as the years passed and political passions cooled, Hoover gained stature and respect in his new role as the Elder Statesman of the nation. His devotion to his country and his love for humanity set him apart. He belonged to his age as a man of incorruptible honor and of a sincerity of purpose that relied on God's help and man's wisdom.

FRANKLIN D. ROOSEVELT

"F.D.R."

ALL WE HAVE to fear is fear itself."

These words, spoken by Franklin D. Roosevelt as he became thirty-second President of the United States on March 4, 1933, gave swift, new hope to a nation bewildered by closing banks and growing breadlines. For the strength of will to overcome adversity, the man who became President that day stood before the country as an inspiration.

People spoke of the great personal struggle that had befallen F.D.R. during the summer of 1921. A robust, handsome man with a brilliant political future, F.D.R. had been stricken with infantile paralysis. Doctors said frankly that they could not be sure whether he would move his legs even after years of patient exercise and treatment. He must face the facts. Cheerfully Roosevelt asked:

"Well, when do we begin?"

Almost everyone believed that the political career of F.D.R. had ended. Even his warmest friend and political advisor, brusque little Louis Howe, gave up hope as he watched the big man struggling to move the muscles in his feet and legs. Then one morning in the spring of 1922 Howe found Roosevelt waiting for him. Large drops of sweat covered his forehead. With a yank of the covers, he pointed to one foot. A grin spread over his face and he shouted:

"Look, Louis! I can wriggle my toe!"

Louis Howe put his doubts aside. He had always known, deep in his heart, that there was a cussed streak in the Roosevelt nature. Like his famous fifth cousin Teddy, F.D.R. had the bounce of three ordinary men. The harder some Roosevelts were slammed, the higher they often vaulted.

Like his fifth cousin, all the advantage of generations of wealth awaited Franklin Delano Roosevelt when he was born on January 30, 1882 at Hyde Park, New York. Until the lad was fourteen private tutors, travel abroad with his parents and a gracious life on the estate at Hyde Park gave him a far from average boyhood. At last James Roosevelt, as indulgent a father as he was a successful railroad executive, consented to send his son to exclusive Groton School to prepare for Harvard. At Groton young Franklin made the football squad, but never won his letter.

A buoyant sense of humor and a lively imagination developed in Franklin Roosevelt during his years at Harvard. As president of the *Crimson*, the college newspaper, he was a crusader for fire escapes on Harvard buildings and for the laying of double duckboards on the gravel walks. But his biggest triumph came in his junior year at the Harvard-Yale football game in New Haven. F.D.R. shipped a linotype machine to New Haven and secretly arranged with a printer to round up fifty carrier boys on bicycles. A special telephone from the Yale field connected him to the office of the printer.

Harvard lost that day, 12 to 0. But the *Crimson* won its biggest scoop over the *Yale News*, for as spectators left the field there were the fifty carrier boys waving copies of the *Crimson* with the score of the game that had just ended!

After Harvard, Roosevelt studied law at Columbia and became a junior partner in a law firm in New York City. When he was offered the Democratic nomination for state senator in a district that was a Republican stronghold in 1910, his jaunty, competitive spirit arose to the challenge. Friends laughed or said in disgust that he had lost his reason—he couldn't win. Experienced politicians ignored him. In an age when an automobile was still a novelty, F.D.R. chugged off in a cloud of dust, carrying his campaign directly to the farmers of the district. He won with a heap of votes to spare.

So once again a Roosevelt reached the State Legislature, owing nothing to the political bosses. In the tradition of Teddy, F.D.R. became a "goo-goo" by opposing a candidate for the United States Senate whom he suspected of being under the thumbs of the bosses. His political career now was like a shooting star, carrying him to the office of Assistant Secretary of the Navy during Wilson's administration and to the nomination as Vice-President on the ticket that unsuccessfully opposed Harding in 1920.

Far from depressed by that defeat, political advisors to F.D.R. were certain he one day would be President. Then came the fateful summer of 1921, the agonizing sickness and paralysis, the years of grim, bitter struggle of a man against his muscles when all hope faded except in the heart of a Louis Howe. In 1928 F.D.R. was ready to try his comeback. He would nominate Al Smith for President.

In New York's Madison Square Garden, where the convention met, F.D.R. stood up on his crutches. His son Jimmy, a strong boy of seventeen, walked with him. They were slow, painful steps, up to the speaker's rostrum. The crowd watched, breathless, spellbound by the intense struggle of the man. One fall, and they would know—he hadn't won the stamina to come back. F.D.R. shuffled forward, smiling, jaunty,

his confidence growing, showing the country for the first time that "all we have to fear is fear itself." Then he stood at the rostrum—alone—and delivered the nominating speech that named Al Smith "the Happy Warrior." Madison Square Garden rocked with a thunderous outburst and Louis Howe said:

"The party hesitated on the verge of a stampede—to Roosevelt!"

In 1928 and in 1930 F.D.R. was elected Governor of New York. As a vote-getter there was a magic in this man. In his programs to develop water power along the St. Lawrence River, to reform prisons, to establish old-age pensions, to put land to more productive use, he captured headlines and the imagination of the voters. He established the first system of state unemployment relief when the depression swept the country. Nominated for President in 1932, he embarked on a vigorous campaign that carried him into thirty-eight states. No one could deny his overwhelming victory over Hoover—by an electoral margin of 472 to 59, by a popular plurality just short of 7,000,000!

Political passions, then and later, divided sharply on F.D.R., and he became saint or sinner, saviour or devil for the same reasons, depending on personal attitudes. Where fifth-cousin Teddy had given the nation "the Square Deal," F.D.R. struggled against the depression by launching "the New Deal."

Unquestionably many of the programs that F.D.R. instituted revolutionized the functions of the Federal Government. Through public work projects, he sought to create jobs for the unemployed. Through public power projects like the Tennessee Valley Administration, he sought to break the grip of holding companies over public utilities which, he maintained, had watered down stocks and raised the rates of electricity to the consumer. An insurance system for small bank deposits, Federal loans to persons threatened with the loss of their homes, a Securities Act which forced those who issued stocks and bonds to tell the full truth about the securities they sold were other examples of F.D.R.'s legislation.

194

Conservative politicians and businessmen charged that the Government under F.D.R. was in the hands of radicals and socialists and dreamy-eyed "brain trusters" whose secret objective was to destroy private enterprise. The people were not convinced. Hard times continued and they looked on F.D.R. as a warm-hearted friend. In the election of 1936 he carried every state except Maine and Vermont and rolled up a popular plurality of 10,000,000 votes.

Stormier days were ahead for F.D.R., however. On the ground that some New Deal agencies were given lawmaking powers which belonged only to Congress, the Supreme Court declared these agencies unconstitutional. The President retaliated in a message to Congress calling for court reforms, including one that would have required the appointment of a younger man to sit with a justice whenever he reached the age of seventy.

In trying to "pack" the court with justices more favorable to New Deal legislation, F.D.R. gave his opponents a new line of attack. He was a dictator, they cried, who wanted to tear up the Constitution. Another, more far-reaching fight was brewing between F.D.R. and those members of Congress who were "isolationists" and who insisted that the Nazi menace under Hitler in Germany was no concern of ours.

By 1940 the Axis partners, Hitler and Mussolini, the dictator of Italy, had gobbled up the small countries of Europe, forced France to her knees, and isolated England. The Jews of Europe had been mercilessly herded into Hitler's concentration camps or put to death in gas chambers. F.D.R.'s policy was to fight the Axis with all measures short of war, but "America First" groups and many professional Republicans opposed him bitterly as a "warmonger" who exaggerated the danger to America.

F.D.R. decided, in the face of the international emergency, to run for an unprecedented third term, and his opponent was Wendell Willkie, an old Bryan Democrat turned Republican, who hammered hard at

F.D.R.'s domestic policies but who refused to let the professionals push him into an attack on the President's foreign policy. Willkie cut Roosevelt's popular plurality to 5,000,000, though F.D.R. carried thirty-eight states with 449 electoral votes against ten states and 82 electoral votes for his opponent.

Events moved swiftly. "We must be the great arsenal of democracy," F.D.R. announced after the election. The following August he met secretly with Prime Minister Churchill aboard a British battleship in Placentine Bay, Newfoundland. From this meeting came the Atlantic Charter, a reaffirmation by the two statesmen of the "four essential human freedoms"—freedom of speech, freedom of religion, freedom from want, freedom from fear—that Roosevelt already had enumerated in his annual message to Congress. Then on December 7, 1941—"a day that shall live in infamy"—Hitler's other Axis partner, Japan, bombed our naval base at Pearl Harbor in Hawaii. America was catapulted, in F.D.R.'s phrase, into "a war of survival."

World War II was a vicious struggle that staggered human imagination. New weapons of destruction spread misery to every corner of the globe. Cities were laid in ruins by long-range bombers. Millions died.

In the "arsenal of democracy," Americans rolled up their sleeves and went to work. Housewives toiled beside soda jerks, riveting wings on bombers, steel sheeting on transports. Around the clock the shipyards, factories, steel mills, mines and farms of America hummed with the labor of men and women determined that human dignity and decency must be restored to the people of the world.

Always in the mind of F.D.R.—and in the mind, too, of Wendell Willkie—was the lesson of World War I when the conflict won on the battlefields had been lost through short-sighted diplomacy. On January 2, 1942 Prime Minister Churchill and F.D.R. gave to the public a bold new fact—a formal document signed by twenty-six governments establishing an international alliance to be known as the United Nations.

The strain of a global war had begun to deepen the lines in the
face of F.D.R. In January, 1943, he traveled to Casablanca to meet with
Churchill. In August they met again at Quebec. In November the President was in Cairo, meeting with Churchill and Generalissimo Chiang
Kai-shek of China. Then he went to Teheran to meet for the first time
with Marshal Joseph Stalin of Russia. At home, with the war still to be
won, F.D.R. decided once again to run for the Presidency. His Republican
opponent, Governor Thomas E. Dewey of New York, picked up a few
more electoral votes than Willkie had in 1940 (Roosevelt, 432 and
Dewey, 99), but F.D.R. increased his popular plurality. Win the war
and win the peace, America said now to a President who had been in
office so long that some who voted had been only children at his first
election.

Two days after F.D.R.'s fourth inauguration in 1945 he left
for Yalta, in the Crimea, to meet once more with Churchill and Stalin.
Victory against Germany was now in sight and "the Big Three" drew
up their final military plans. Plans also were made for an organization
meeting of the United Nations in San Francisco. Grave problems for
settling the boundary of Poland and governing defeated Germany —
problems that still haunt the minds of freedom-loving people — were
solved in a good faith that then seemed reasonable. On his way home
the President conferred with the Kings of Egypt and Saudi Arabia and
the Emperor of Ethiopia.

A very tired F.D.R. went to rest at a favorite retreat, the "Little White House," in Warm Springs, Georgia. Foremost in his mind now was the approaching meeting of the United Nations in San Francisco. The challenge that confronted the world he stated boldly:

"We must cultivate the science of human relations—the ability of all peoples, of all kinds, to live together and work together in the same world, at peace."

These were the last words written by F.D.R. On April 12, 1945 — eighty-three days after his fourth inauguration—a cerebral hemorrhage ended his life. A shocked nation, a shocked world, received the news of his death with a feeling of personal loss such as people had experienced at the time of Lincoln's assassination.

Political friend and foe alike realized that a man had passed away whose impact upon the nation and the world had forever changed our common destiny. No man in all American history ever had been more deeply loved or more scurrilously abused. The attacks of those who hated the man were extended to his wife, Eleanor Roosevelt, who so often had been his legs and eyes and personal messenger in traveling around a country gripped by depression and a world stricken by a war of survival. But in 1946 Mrs. Roosevelt took her seat as a delegate to the United Nations. This time the dream of a wartime President for a fellowship of nations to solve their disputes had endured.

The White House that to William Howard Taft had proved "the lonesomest place in the world" to F.D.R. became the stormiest. In a democracy all political opinions must be free to speak out boldly, even abusively. The people listen, weigh the arguments, and on election day behind a drawn curtain make a decision in the privacy of their individual consciences. This is the American democratic process—the victory of freedom—the reason for a White House and a President. That F.D.R. remained President longer than any other man in history resulted from a simple fact. The American people chose to keep him in office.

198

HARRY S. TRUMAN
"Statesman of the Atomic Age"

W ITHIN FOUR HOURS after Roosevelt's death, Harry S.
Truman took the oath of office as thirty-third President of the
United States. Never would the world witness a more dramatic illustra-
tion of the strength of a democracy that, engaged in an enormous global
war, could change the administration of its government without loss of
stride in its war effort and without a ripple in the confidence of the
people that the nation would endure. As the seventh man to reach the
Presidency through the accident of death, Truman did not mistake the
colossal problems that confronted him. To reporters he said:

"If you fellows ever pray, pray for me."

The nation prayed for Harry S. Truman, recognizing the courage
of heart and mind he would need for the staggering tasks ahead. What
the people saw when they beheld the new President on television or in
newsreels was a friendly man who looked like a neighbor living down

the street. The facts of the career that had brought Truman to the highest office in the land were certainly unexceptional. At thirty-seven he had been a failure in the haberdashery business in Kansas City and now, weeks short of his sixty-first birthday, he was President.

Life for Harry S. Truman began on May 8, 1884 in the little Missouri town of Lamar. For over a century his ancestors had been farmers and stanch Baptists, and young Harry grew up as Missouri farm boys usually do—taking the day's chores as a matter of duty, attending the local schools, swimming, fishing, getting along with a crowd. Weak eyesight kept Harry from entering West Point, but he took luck as it came and wasn't afraid of hard work. A timekeeper on the Santa Fe Railroad, a lad wrapping papers for the Kansas City *Star*, a bank clerk and bookkeeper—these were the jobs behind him when, at twenty-two he returned home to run the farm for his widowed mother.

In Lamar during World War I the bands thumped "Over There" and "It's a Grand Old Flag," and Harry Truman put on a khaki uniform and sailed overseas to do his share in making the world safe for democracy. He was in the thick of the dirty fighting at Saint-Mihiel and the Argonne and came home a major in the field artillery. The unsuccessful venture in the haberdashery business followed.

The Democratic political boss of Kansas City in those days was "Big Tom" Pendergast, whose scandalous dealings finally landed him in a penitentiary. In Harry Truman, "Big Tom" recognized an affable vote-getter, and the Pendergast machine pushed Truman steadily ahead in politics—as overseer of highways in Missouri's Jackson County, as a county judge, and then in 1934 as a United States Senator.

Six years later "Big Tom's" political dynasty began to sink in the sands of scandal. Yet Truman stood above the machine—as honest as his devout Baptist parents, a hard worker who had studied nights at the Kansas City School of Law while serving as a county judge—and though Missourians sent "Big Tom" to his political grave, they returned Truman

to the Senate. Soon as chairman of the Senate Committee to Investigate the National Defense Program—popularly known as the Truman Committee—the farm boy from Missouri began to win his first real national recognition. As the campaign of 1944 approached, the stand taken by Vice-President Henry Wallace on civil liberties made him a storm-center among Southern Democrats and so the nomination as F.D.R.'s running mate went to Truman.

Events now moved with cyclonic speed for the farm boy from Missouri. Eighty-three days after Truman assumed his quiet role as presiding officer of the Senate, Roosevelt died. Four hours later Truman was leader of a nation at war. Twenty-seven days later he announced the unconditional surrender of Germany. The next month he was at Potsdam, meeting with Churchill and Stalin, and announcing the Potsdam Declaration that called for the unconditional surrender of Japan. Then on August 6, 1945 (our time) a lone American bomber flew over the Japanese city of Hiroshima.

Sunny skies smiled down on the 343,000 inhabitants of Hiroshima that pleasant August day. At this point of the war people shrugged at the sight of a single enemy plane. A reconnaissance flight—what difference did it make? Then a single bomb fell to earth. A great ball of fire climbed into a sky suddenly turned unreal by a bluish-green light. When the smoke, dust, and fire disappeared, that one bomb had devasted an area of four square miles. The Japanese dead numbered 78,150, the missing 13,933, the burned and wounded 37,425, the homeless and sick 176,987.

"We have spent two billion dollars on the greatest scientific gamble in history — and won," President Truman declared on this day when the Atomic Age was born.

The average mind, however, could not quickly grasp this new source of power. In Japan a second atomic bomb dropped on the city of Nagasaki three days later brought the war lords to their knees. When, on September 2, 1945, aboard the *U.S.S. Missouri* in Tokyo Bay the articles of formal surrender were signed, in many American hearts uneasiness mixed with exultation. War had become so terrible that the meetings in San Francisco that had resulted in the organization of the United Nations acquired deeper meaning. On the day when the Charter of the United Nations had been adopted, President Truman had told the delegates in San Francisco: "What a great day this can be in history!" After Hiroshima, Americans realized what a great day it *must* be.

Wars, always ending raggedly, confronted the nation with the problems of readjustment to peace. Factories found war contracts swiftly canceled and workers lost their overtime pay. Strikes and demands by businessmen for an end to price controls and other wartime restrictions produced grave disruptions. At the President's order, the Federal Government temporarily seized railroads, packing houses and coal mines. Truman, still a Senator at heart, formulated policies to meet the new domestic emergencies, but relied on Congress to enact the necessary legislation. Members of Congress, representing many conflicting interests, failed to accept the leadership thrust upon it.

Although the predicted widespread unemployment did not develop and the nation's production increased despite strikes, political experts gave Truman no chance of winning re-election in 1948. Governor Thomas E. Dewey of New York was again the Republican candidate, and conducted his campaign as though he already had won. Governor Dewey, however, failed to convince one man that he was a sure winner. His name was Harry S. Truman. Wise to the political strength in holding together the farm and labor vote, Truman traveled 31,000 miles and made over 350 speeches as he took the campaign to the people, blasting away at the Republican Eightieth Congress as a "do nothing" Congress, and obviously enjoying the rough and tumble of politics. So, too, did the people—at least the 23,600,000 who voted for Truman, giving him 304 electoral votes and a second term.

Among the most significant events of Truman's next four years was the signing in Washington on April 4, 1949 of the North Atlantic Treaty Organization (NATO), when the United States, Canada, Great Britain, France, the Netherlands, Belgium, Luxembourg, Italy, Norway, Denmark, Iceland and Portugal reaffirmed their adherence to the Charter of the United Nations and pledged to "unite their efforts for collective defense and for the preservation of peace and security" by considering armed aggression against any one member an attack on all. The hot war just ended had drifted into the "cold war," when the free nations of the world stood against the aggressions of Communism.

At Potsdam in 1948 the Allied Powers had agreed that the thirty-eighth parallel would divide Soviet-dominated North Korea from the Republic of South Korea. But the Potsdam pledge was broken on June 25, 1950 when North Koreans invaded the land to the south. Truman acted quickly, ordering General Douglas MacArthur to command United Nations forces in a savage war that once more filled American newspapers with casualty lists. MacArthur pushed the Communist aggressors back beyond the thirty-eighth parallel, and in November American troops reached the Manchurian border. But when, as Commander-in-chief, Truman stopped MacArthur from carrying the conflict into Communist China, whose "volunteers" had entered the war, the General and President provided a future squabble between Republicans and Democrats.

Another source of intense controversy was the Taft-Hartley Labor Act, which demanded a period of mediation before a strike could be called and imposed other restrictions on labor. Truman vetoed the act but Congress passed it again.

Approaching the age of sixty-eight as his second term ended, Truman was ready to leave the White House. In the role of an ex-President he has become an American image—the affable, smiling, happy "Man from Independence" who understands politics and believes that he owes no apology for his actions as President.

204

DWIGHT D. EISENHOWER

"Ike"

I LIKE IKE" chanted the 33,936,252 Americans who, going to the polls in 1952 to vote for Dwight D. Eisenhower, gave him a plurality of more than 6,500,000 as he became thirty-fourth President of the United States. The members of the medical board at West Point who had considered Eisenhower's case in 1915, wondering if the wrenched knee he had sustained playing football made him a suitable candidate for an army commission, could be glad now they had taken a chance on smiling, friendly Ike.

Ike, then twenty-five years of age, looked back on a life that had begun on October 14, 1890 in Denison, Texas. His ancestors were devout Germans who had fled to Switzerland to escape religious persecution in the 1600's, then had migrated to Pennsylvania a century later, and finally had traveled by covered wagon to Kansas. Here in the town of

Abilene were the real roots of the Eisenhower family. Ike was only two when the family returned to Kansas. Almost by accident he became the first Texan to occupy the White House.

As a construction engineer, Ike's father had rough times, financially, raising a family of six sons (a seventh died in infancy), yet he reared them all to respect hard work and the deep religious convictions of the Church of the Brethren in Christ. A President of the United States, a college president, a successful lawyer, banker, engineer, and business-man—certainly the Eisenhower parents had no need to apologize for how their six sons built careers upon the foundation of their home training.

Ike grew up, a normal boy in Abilene. In high school he played football and baseball, and for a year after graduation knocked around at odd jobs. He wanted an appointment to the Naval Academy at Annapolis, but had passed the age limit of twenty, so off he went to West Point, thereafter an army man at heart. In his sophomore year he understudied for Geoffrey Keyes, the Point's great halfback. Ike was good. He could tackle so that an opponent stayed tackled, as even Carlisle's immortal Jim Thorpe discovered. In six games Ike kept coming, showing the promise of a star at the Point. Then a broken knee ended his career on the gridiron, and almost his future as an army man.

Early in Ike's career he was marked as one of those "mechanized nuts" who refused to talk anything but tank warfare and air power. During World War I he was raised to temporary rank as a lieutenant colonel and commanded the 6,000 men of the Tank Corps at Camp Colt in Gettysburg, Pennsylvania, but in 1920 he was reduced to major, and there his rank stuck, in a groove, for the next sixteen years. Meanwhile Ike served in responsible capacities at army posts in New Jersey, Georgia and Maryland, as executive director of Camp Gaillard in the Canal Zone, as an assistant executive to the Assistant Secretary of War, and then as an aide to the Chief of Staff, General Douglas MacArthur.

Ike and MacArthur worked well as a team, whether hammering at Congress for the means to build a bigger, better mechanized army or in the Philippines, strengthening our defenses there. Air-minded Ike decided he wanted to fly, and at forty-five qualified for his pilot's license. The organization of the Philippine Air Force, the establishment of the Philippine Military Academy and the designing of secret airfields were all Eisenhower accomplishments. At the outbreak of World War II, Ike was stationed at San Antonio, Texas as Chief of Staff of the Third Army. Five days after Pearl Harbor he was summoned to Washington to do the thinking for the war-plans division of our military forces.

Upon the shoulders of two old army friends, Ike and MacArthur, suddenly rested America's hopes of winning a global war. In May, 1942, with 10,000 Americans and 45,000 Filipinos becoming prisoners of Japan with the fall of Bataan, MacArthur left the Philippines with the promise that one day he would be back. And in June, Ike left for London to work almost around the clock as he coordinated the Allied movements that drove the Nazis out of North Africa. His next plan knocked Italy out of the war with the invasion of Sicily. Back in England Ike now coordinated and commanded the greatest military invasion in history — "Operation Overlord."

In the misty dawn of June 6, 1944, off the beaches of Normandy, Allied battleships opened their guns. Overhead zoomed waves of Allied planes, dotting the hostile coastline with the orange flames of exploding bombs. And then game young men from practically every town and crossroads in America—lads in khaki who called themselves G. I. Joe—waded from their barges and hit the beaches, spread-eagled, there to stay or die. Within five days eighty miles of Normandy coast were held by sixteen Allied divisions and the push was on that, on May 2, 1945, carried Ike and his G. I.'s to the surrender of Berlin.

With the exception of George Washington, if every military hero in American history could have been rolled into one idol, they could not have claimed greater affection and respect than the American people now bestowed on Dwight David Eisenhower. Both major parties jockeyed for Ike as a potential presidential candidate, but he seemed to turn his back on this ambition when, in 1947, he became President of Columbia University.

Senator Robert Taft of Ohio, who was certain he would be as happy in the White House as his father had been lonely and dejected, was swept aside as Ike finally committed himself to the Republicans and the Eisenhower boom grew. In 1952 against Adlai Stevenson, the Democratic candidate, Ike rolled up an electoral vote plurality of 442 to 89.

As the third regular army man to reach the White House, Ike had no greater political experience than his strictly military predecessors. Some campaign promises he could fulfill, but history in action has a way of confounding campaign orators. Crises arise that demand solution, most of all in a world of "the cold war" where freedom is imperiled by a system supported by slave labor and low standards of living.

Yet Ike seized many opportunities for dynamic leadership. The Strategic Air Command, equipped with atomic bombs, was designed to give America a striking force that would discourage future global war. At Panmunjom in July, 1953, he fulfilled his pledge to end the Korean War that had cost the nation 33,237 dead and 103,376 wounded. Legislation was passed to limit any future President to two terms in office—proof to F.D.R. "New Dealers" that even in politics all things come to him who waits. Under Senator Joseph McCarthy of Wisconsin charges of Communist infiltration in government often reached extremes, resulting in a controversy between McCarthy and Army Secretary Robert T. Stevens that fascinated millions of Americans when the hearings were televised for thirty-six days in 1954. The Senate later censored McCarthy for his undignified conduct.

History frequently turns unexpected corners. In the United States Supreme Court, Monday is a day of decision. Rarely had the country

Stanley Dersh

been so electrified by any ruling of the Court as on May 17, 1954 when Chief Justice Earl Warren read in a quiet voice the unanimous opinion in the case of *Brown v. Board of Education*:

"We conclude that in the field of public education the doctrine of 'separate but equal' has no place. Separate educational facilities are inherently unequal. Therefore, we hold that the plaintiffs and other similarly situated for whom the actions have been brought are, by reason of the segregation complained of, deprived of the equal protection of the laws guaranteed by the Fourteenth Amendment."

Again, for Ike personally history turned an unexpected corner when, in 1955, the nation learned with shock that the President had suffered a heart attack, and all Americans rejoiced at his recovery. Still another unexpected corner turned by history was the announcement in 1957 that, by using rocket propulsion, the Russians had placed their "Sputnik" in orbit in outer space. Soon American scientists had also launched manmade satellites. Full statehood was granted to Alaska and Hawaii.

In 1956, running against Adlai Stevenson, Ike easily won a second term as President, and when four years later he reached his 70th birthday he became the first occupant of the White House to attain that age. The hope for a new era of world peace was sorely blasted when Soviet Premier Nikita Khrushchev broke off a meeting of world leaders in Paris in May, 1960. Ike returned home to a welcome of 200,000 persons, who lined the streets of Washington and cheered this man of good will. The high esteem in which he was held by his countrymen was unchanged.

Retiring to his farm in Gettysburg, Pennsylvania, after his tenure as President, Ike nevertheless remained influential in world affairs and his counsel was sought by three White House successors. Repeated heart attacks and hospital confinement during most of his last year of life could not daunt his vibrant spirit, aptly expressed by his own words as he awaited death: "I've always loved my wife. I've always loved my children. I've always loved my grandchildren. I've always loved my country."

JOHN F. KENNEDY
"J. F. K."

JACK KENNEDY was never afraid to speak his mind when he believed he was right. Once, as a boy, he addressed a note to his father: "My recent allowance is 40¢. This I used for aeroplanes and other playthings of childhood but now I am a scout and I put away my childish things. Before I would spend 20¢ of my 40¢ allowance and in five minutes I would have empty pockets and nothing to gain and 20¢ to lose. When I am a scout I have to buy canteens, haversacks, blankets, searchlicgs, poncho things that will last for years and I can always use it while I can't use chocolate marshmallow sunday ice cream and so I put in my plea for a raise of thirty cents for me to buy schut things and pay my own way around. . . ."

If Jack received his raise—and the chances are he did—his ability as a speller wasn't one of the reasons. But the Kennedys, a large family, have always had a way of sticking together in times of need, whether the occasion was meeting the requirements of a good Boy Scout or becoming the youngest man and the first Roman Catholic ever elected President of the United States.

Born in Brookline, Massachusetts on May 29, 1917, the second of nine children, John Fitzgerald Kennedy grew up in a family that often lived, slept and ate "politics." Grandfather Patrick Kennedy was known in Boston as a shrewd old Democratic ward boss who had won election to the Massachusetts legislature. By trade he was a saloonkeeper—or what, in the phrase of Boston blue bloods, was called "Shanty Irish"—but he knew how to handle people. On Jack's mother's side, Grandfather John F. Fitzgerald was the renowned "Honey Fitz" who held many elective offices—in the Massachusetts legislature, in congress, and as mayor of Boston. By the time these two families merged to produce, among their numerous clan, a future President, the Kennedys had climbed up the Boston social ladder to become "Lace Curtain Irish." In 1917, when Jack howled his presence into the world, his father, Joseph P. Kennedy, was already well on his way to amassing a huge fortune through such enterprises as banking, motion pictures and the stock market.

So Jack grew up in a household where, day in, day out, things were popping. These were happy years, first in Brookline and later in Riverdale and Bronxville, New York, where Jack romped and played and plugged his way through the first six grades of school. Older brother Joe was a bit bossy, but Jack managed to survive this bout of normal childhood tyranny, and his pet of the family was his sister "Kick," whose given name was Kathleen. Both would be killed in later years—Joe in World War II, "Kick" in a plane crash in France.

But these were tragedies of the future when, at the age of thirteen, Jack started going away to school. He was not a great "scholar" at the Canterbury School in New Milford, Connecticut, where he went out for football "practice," muddled through Latin within an eyewink of flunking, and learned to swim fifty yards in thirty seconds. He was sent to another Connecticut institution — Choate School in Wallingford — where he added French to Latin among his scholastic bugaboos, proved only fair in English and history, and graduated 64th in a class of 112.

But the Kennedy smile, the Kennedy personality must have been working even then, for his classmates voted him the "most likely to succeed."

In part because Papa Joe and Brother Joe were both Harvard men, Jack decided to be different and entered Princeton. A summer in London was spoiled by illness—a recurring nuisance all through Jack's life—and illness also interrupted his studies at Princeton. So he wound up at Harvard after all, earning a string of C's in most subjects, until all at once in his junior year he seemed to find himself. Since his father now was ambassador to Great Britain, appointed by President Franklin D. Roosevelt, it was natural for Jack to spend another summer in Europe. The ignorance of almost all Americans in European events affecting their lives impressed him most. The idea stuck with him, grew, and became enormously important in his future.

Jack graduated from Harvard in 1940—with honors in political science — and from London his father cabled: "TWO THINGS I ALWAYS KNEW ABOUT YOU ONE THAT YOU ARE SMART TWO THAT YOU ARE A SWELL GUY." Jack's senior thesis, a study of England's political weaknesses before World War II, he rewrote into a book, *While England Slept*, and it became a best-seller. Rejected by the army because of previous injuries sustained playing football, Jack was determined to find a place with the American fighting forces in World War II. For five months he followed a program of exercises to strengthen his back, and in 1942 he received his commission in the navy.

On the night of August 2nd of the following year, Jack was in command of a PT boat in Blackett Strait, west of New Georgia, one of the Solomon Islands in the South Pacific. Out of the darkness appeared the Japanese destroyer *Amagiri*.

Helplessly, Jack watched as the destroyer sliced his PT boat like a knife cutting a loaf of bread into halves. Jack's ability as a swimmer, which he had first revealed as a lad at the Canterbury School, helped now to save his life and the lives of ten other survivors from his boat. He guided his men to a Japanese-held island, then led them across barracuda-infested waters to still another island where he found friendly natives. On a coconut shell he carved the message: "ELEVEN ALIVE NATIVE KNOWS POSIT AND REEFS NAURU ISLAND KENNEDY."

In time, Jack and his men were rescued, and he received both the Purple Heart and the Navy and Marine Corps Medal for this exploit. But these were small comfort in the grim days ahead. Malaria and a reinjury to his back were only part of his misery. The deeper wound was in his heart—the news that Brother Joe had been killed in Europe.

Discharged from the navy in 1945, Jack served a brief stint as a newspaper reporter, then turned to politics as a candidate for congress. His family and friends threw themselves into the campaign and Jack won easily. In Washington, he soon became known as a hard worker who dug deeply into the background of any legislation he supported (his special interests were housing and labor), and everyone realized that this good-looking young man with a mind of his own was going places. And go he did in 1952, winning a seat in the United States Senate against Henry Cabot Lodge. The following year he married beautiful Jacqueline Lee Bouvier—certainly here was a young man sitting on top of the world.

But poor health still plagued him and twice during 1954-55 Jack was hospitalized. Yet even on his back, Jack kept forging ahead, working on his book, *Profiles in Courage*, that in 1957 won the Pulitzer Prize in history. The year before he had come within a few votes of gaining the Democratic nomination for Vice President, and now there was something in the air that seemed to say: "Watch Kennedy. He means to be elected President in 1960."

Well, so he was. The odds were heavily stacked against him. He was attacked because he was young, a Roman Catholic, a rich man's son. Old professionals in his party were committed to their own favorite candidates. And in Vice President Richard M. Nixon, the obvious Republican candidate, he would face a formidable opponent.

Kennedy won a clear victory in the electoral college, 303 to 219, but his margin in the popular vote was razor-edge thin. In his inaugural address, the new President, a youthful, vigorous 43, challenged the people, "Ask not what your country can do for you — ask what you can do for your country."

He held the toughest job in the world. A Communist-style government in Cuba, the building of the Berlin wall, the resumption of nuclear testing by Russia, and political trouble in South Vietnam were proof that the cold war had not subsided. Kennedy reacted with the strength of a bold, imaginative leader. His Alliance for Progress offered money to the countries of Latin America if they would help themselves in improving their social conditions. Peace Corps volunteers assisted under-developed countries in becoming self-sufficient. Russian-built missiles, capable of striking the United States, were being mounted on launching pads in Cuba. When Kennedy ordered a naval blockade and mobilization of armed forces, Soviet Premier Nikita Khrushchev had the rocket bases dismantled and the missiles returned to Russia. Later, international tension seemed to ease, and most nations signed a nuclear test-ban.

A spectacular achievement at home during Kennedy's years in the Presidency was the space flights of astronauts like John Glenn and Scott Carpenter. In May, 1962, the President told Congress, "I believe that this nation should commit itself to achieving the goal, before this decade is out, of landing a man on the moon and returning him safely to earth." Civil rights demonstrations, especially in Mississippi and Alabama, found the President firm in his faith that all citizens should enjoy equal opportunities and protection under the law. Joyous crowds greeted Kennedy when he visited Dallas, Texas, on November 22, 1963. But as a motorcade bore him through the city, shots were heard. Struck in back and head, the President slumped forward. He had been mortally wounded. A grief-stricken nation gave him a hero's funeral which was attended by heads of government from all corners of the globe.

LYNDON B. JOHNSON
"All the Way with LBJ"

GOD REIGNS, and the government at Washington still lives," said James A. Garfield on the morning that Abraham Lincoln died. In this spirit, ninety-eight minutes after President Kennedy's death from an assassin's bullet, Lyndon Baines Johnson, standing in the cabin of the Presidential airplane at Love Field, Dallas, became the thirty-sixth President of the United States. Near him stood Jacqueline Kennedy, her suit still stained with the blood of her martyred husband. The oath of office was administered by Judge Sarah T. Hughes; her eyes were red from weeping.

"Okay," the new President said with the decisiveness so characteristic of him. "Let's get this plane back to Washington."

His first official act was to write personal letters to the Kennedy children.

The country was thoroughly familiar with this lanky, six-foot-three Texan whose favorite quotation, taken from Isaiah, is: "Come now, let us reason together." Thirty-two of his fifty-five years already had been devoted to the public service of the nation. "I have seen five Presidents fill this awesome office," he told the country in his Thanksgiving Day address. "I have known them well, and I've counted them all as friends." Indeed, the ability to get along with people was the trait which, above all others, had brought Lyndon Baines Johnson to the forefront in the sometimes "rough-and-tumble" game of national politics. Never was this talent more obvious than in 1957 when, as majority leader, he piloted through the Senate the first civil rights bill to be passed in over eighty years.

Born August 27, 1908, in a farmhouse in Stonewall, Texas, Lyndon Johnson was raised in a "get-up-and-go" atmosphere. His grandfather and father—both named Sam—served in the Texas Legislature, and Granddaddy Johnson, impressed by Lyndon, predicted: "He'll be a United States senator some day." The boy certainly was not afraid of work. At nine, he earned his pocket money shining shoes in Johnson City's solitary barber shop; at fifteen, he completed high school. Wanderlust led him to California where he did any job that came his way—elevator operator, car washer, handyman in a cafe. He tried to study law there, but that was not to be. So Lyndon Johnson returned to Johnson City and secured a job with a road-building gang.

"It became increasingly apparent to me," he said in later years, "that there was something to this idea of higher education." He borrowed seventy-five dollars, hitchhiked to San Marcos, Texas, and enrolled in Southwest State Teachers College. Again, he was willing to take any odd job that would pay his way. He worked as part-time janitor, door-to-door hosiery salesman, and secretary to the college president. In three and a half years, he received his Bachelor of Science degree.

Before graduating, he dropped out of college for lack of funds and taught for a year in the Mexican school in tiny Cotulla, the county seat of La Salle County, Texas. He was a dedicated teacher, improving dramatically the education of the Mexican children there. "Mr.

Johnson" insisted that his thirty-two pupils learn, "inspiring" them with spankings if their homework was not done. He even confronted the local school board to get sports and games equipment for them, and battled to have baseball games and track meets scheduled, as at other schools in the district.

Following college, Lyndon, at age twenty-two, hustled off to Houston to teach public speaking and debating in one of the city's high schools. But politics was in his blood; and in 1931, he left the classroom to serve as secretary to Representative Richard M. Kleberg of Texas. There was a bustle to Lyndon—when he was around, things were done and done fast—and that went for courtship, too. Within six weeks after he met Claudia Alta Taylor, the daughter of a wealthy Texas rancher who had been nicknamed "Lady Bird" by her nurse, the couple were married. Two fine daughters, Lynda Bird and Lucy Baines, added to the liveliness of a household where Papa popped in and out as he advanced his whirlwind career in politics.

In Washington, people began talking about this young Texas fireball. Shrewd Congressman Sam Rayburn, who had served with Lyndon's father in the legislature back home, recognized a "chip off the old block."

As Kleberg's assistant, one of Johnson's most rewarding achievements was persuading the newly-formed Federal Land Bank to offer mortgage guarantees to every one of sixty-seven failing farms in south

Texas. He persuaded the Land Bank, a newly-created agency of Franklin Roosevelt's "New Deal," to advance the financing against future crops. Young Johnson thought up this innovative means of securing mortgages against soil productivity.

Another shrewd judge of leaders, President Franklin D. Roosevelt, also liked the cut of this fellow, and in 1935, appointed him Texas State Administrator of the National Youth Administration. After two years, the Texan resigned to run for Congress. He defeated nine other candidates—LBJ was on his way. A member of the Naval Reserve, he became the first Congressman to enter active service in World War II, and won the Silver Star for gallantry in action on a flight over enemy emplacements in New Guinea. He had risen to the rank of lieutenant commander when, after a year, FDR ordered all Congressmen in the armed services to return to their legislative duties.

Lyndon Johnson served five successive terms in the House before he fulfilled Granddaddy Johnson's prophecy by running for the Senate in 1948. His opponent was Governor Coke Stevenson, and the future President won by a slim majority of 87 out of the 988,295 votes cast, but in 1954, when he stood for re-election, he won overwhelmingly. There was a flair to Lyndon Johnson that people liked. Two years earlier, when he became leader of the Senate at the age of forty-four, he was the youngest man ever to achieve that honor. His mania for affixing "LBJ" to everything—his cuff-links, the initials of his wife and daughters, the name of his ranch in Texas—became a source of national amusement. His average working day of eighteen hours left some colleagues wondering if he ever did sleep. In 1955, he suffered a severe heart attack. Just how much this affliction was going to slow down LBJ became questionable when, that summer, he had a telephone and mimeograph machine moved into his hospital room. In time, he was back to what he would regard as a curtailed working day of only sixteen hours. By 1960, he was ready to plunge into a rugged primary fight with Kennedy for the

Democratic Presidential nomination. Johnson's catchy campaign slogan of "All the way with LBJ" certainly captured the imagination, but Kennedy won easily on the first ballot, 806 votes to 409, then surprised the Democratic convention by announcing that he wanted Lyndon Johnson for his running mate.

As Vice President, Johnson worked quietly, modestly, efficiently. He served as Chairman of the National Aeronautics and Space Agency and of the Committee on Equal Employment Opportunity. Untiring and unstinting in giving of his strength and his abilities, he traveled to many foreign countries as the President's representative. His loyalty to Kennedy, no matter what issue was involved, was unflinching, and Kennedy left no doubt in the public mind that, when he ran for re-election, he still wished to have Lyndon Johnson by his side.

Perhaps what the country came to admire most in Vice President Johnson was his intense loyalty. He could love deeply—country, president, party. On that gloomy day in 1945 when FDR died, he did not hide his tears. "There are plenty of us," he said, "left here to try and run interference, but the man who carried the ball is gone—gone." He did not deny his sense of personal loss, "He was just like a daddy to me always." A little more than eighteen years separated this tearful utterance from that sunny November 22, 1963, in Dallas when the shots of an assassin ended the life of John F. Kennedy. The grief that stabbed all of America was like a knife thrust in Lyndon Johnson's heart. Once President Eisenhower had said to him, pointing to the chair behind the desk in the White House, "Some day you'll be sitting in that chair." Lyndon Johnson had smiled and answered, "No, Mr. President, that's one chair I'll never sit in."

But history decided otherwise, and two days after a grieving nation had paid its last tribute to John F. Kennedy, a new president spoke to a joint session of Congress and to the American people. "The time has come," Lyndon Johnson said, "for Americans of all races and creeds and political beliefs to understand and to respect one another. So, let us put an end to the teaching and the preaching of hate and evil and violence. Let us turn away from the fanatics, from the far left and the far right, from the apostles of bitterness and bigotry, from those defiant of law, and those who pour venom into our nation's bloodstream."

No one could bring back John F. Kennedy, forget him, or forgive the cruel act of his assassination. Tributes to his memory would be many—indeed, President Johnson would soon give the new name of Cape Kennedy to Cape Canaveral as one such tribute.

The "Johnson touch" soon became apparent as the tall Texan took over command of the White House. A superb politician, he used the telephone and personal meetings with legislators "up on The Hill" to drive through laws he believed were essential in achieving the "Great Society." And results followed: in February, 1964, he obtained passage of a federal income tax reduction bill; in April he settled a five-year-old railroad work-rules dispute; next, his "War on Poverty" received overwhelming Congressional support by the passage of legislation providing (a) work-training programs to reduce the number of school drop-outs, (b) work-study programs to help needy college students, (c) community anti-poverty projects, and (d) loans to farmers and low-income business people. A crowning success of these early months in the Presidency was the passage of the Civil Rights Act of 1964 which outlawed discrimination in public places, employment and voting rights.

Johnson's popularity grew as from day to day his own style of Texas personality emerged. News pictures showed him turning off unnecessary lights in the White House as a symbol of his drive for economy in government. With his favorite beagles on a leash, he walked the legs off reporters as he conducted press conferences "on the run." Washington haberdashers began to stock Western hats from the same company in Garland, Texas, that supplied the President's hats.

The Republicans nominated conservative Senator Barry Goldwater of Arizona to oppose Johnson in the 1964 presidential elections. The GOP candidate, in attacking the Civil Rights Act as unconstitutional, and the entire Johnson program of social legislation as a ruse to concentrate more and more power in the central government, shouted himself into hoarseness; Johnson, smiling, replied gently that the nation's economic health had never been better and that his was the party that loved all the people, without regard to wealth, creed or color. The result followed the unbelievable predictions of expert forecasters: Johnson won 486 electoral votes to Goldwater's 52; his popular vote of 43,121,085 was the greatest ever given a presidential candidate in American history.

Lyndon Johnson continued to sweep his domestic program through Congress and as he neared the close of his second year in office he could say exultantly: "We've passed seventy-five major bills so far. Back in the '30's, . . . they'd get five." The pattern of his domestic policies remained determined, unbreakable: a declaration of open warfare against the Ku Klux Klan in support of civil rights; stringent pressure on industry to keep wages and profits in balance so as to avoid inflation; a vigorous expansion of his program to reduce poverty through the Job Corps and other agencies.

But LBJ's stubborn insistence on escalating the Vietnam War to where it cost more than 40,000 American deaths could not easily be passed off with a joke: "You can shoot a Texas Ranger, but he just keeps coming on." Civilians and Congressmen alike were split into factions: those who favored the war were termed "hawks," and those who did not were "doves." All ages, from teenagers to grandparents, were involved. Although quick military intervention in the Dominican Republic probably saved that country from a communistic form of government and delicate diplomatic disputes with Panama were adjusted, LBJ's popularity slipped rapidly. People claimed that money needed for domestic improvements was being wasted senselessly in Asia. During that time, more than a hundred cities were ravaged by interracial riots and the great black leader and Nobel Peace Prize winner, Dr. Martin Luther King, Jr., was assassinated. Senator Robert F. Kennedy of New York, brother of the preceding President, broke with Johnson regarding the course of

the ship of state in a White House argument as early as March, 1967. A year later, Lyndon Johnson unexpectedly announced to the nation on television and radio that he no longer sought re-election.

Other candidates from the Senate, supporting the "dove" position, challenged Vice-President Hubert H. Humphrey, the "heir apparent," for the Democratic nomination for President. Senator Robert Kennedy made his bid and, campaigning strongly in the primaries, forged toward becoming front-runner, but just as he carried the California and South Dakota primaries, he also was assassinated. Humphrey, softening his stand on Vietnam, came on with a rush. But he was too late. As one television commentator said, anyone who got the Democratic nomination following the resignation of a president and the assassination of a major candidate carried "a tarnished shield."

President Johnson retired to his Austin, Texas, ranch to manage his vast financial empire, enjoy his grandchildren, and write his memoirs. Then, on January 22, 1973, the man who had spent his entire adulthood making life better for all people in the United States, died of a heart attack at his ranch.

RICHARD M. NIXON

"The Professional Politician"

POLITICS was the passion of Richard Milhous Nixon. After twenty-two years in and out of elected office, including two terms as Vice President to Dwight D. Eisenhower, he became the first Republican to win the Presidency in eighteen years.

At fifty-six years of age, he was elected to the office by a margin of popular votes that was almost razor-thin. His victory over Democratic candidate Hubert Humphrey and his running mate, Maine's Senator Edward Muskie, was further narrowed by a third party ticket consisting of Alabama's ex-governor George Corley Wallace and Curtis Emerson Lemay, retired Air Force Chief of Staff. Not since Woodrow Wilson, who also emerged the victor in a three party battle, had the margin been so small; Wilson's percentage being 41.9 of the popular vote, to Nixon's 43.4 percent.

Despite his minimal plurality win of the popular vote, his electoral college victory was substantial—carrying 302 of 538 votes. Attainment of the Presidency was a life-long dream for the boy whose mother and grandmother told him he was destined to do great things. Born January 9, 1913, to Quaker parents in the farm community of Yorba Linda, California, Richard Nixon was the third and most ambitious of four sons. His parents, Frank and Hannah, moved the family to Whittier, California when the boys were very young, and their father ran a grocery store there. After completing high school with honors, young Richard hoped to go east to attend Harvard or Yale. But in 1930, during the Great Depression, the Nixons' financial situation did not allow it. So he attended Whittier college on a trust fund his grandfather had established, and went on to Duke University Law School on money he borrowed from his father, graduating third in his class.

Six years before, after an unsuccessful bid for the governorship of California, Nixon had told the press point-blank that: "they wouldn't have Dick Nixon to kick around anymore." His election to the Presidency was the result of a well-timed political comeback that was based, in part, on the "new image" of Richard Nixon—one which concentrated on a better presentation for television and the media, as well as a more congenial manner.

Candidate Nixon made a conscious effort to throw off the hard-boiled personality he had projected in his earlier years in office. As co-author of the Anti-Communist bill of 1948, which propelled the young Congressman to prominence on the House Un-American Activities Committee, his relentless investigation led to the perjury conviction of Alger Hiss, a former State Department official charged with passing classified information to foreign agents. In his 1950 Senate race he branded his opponent, Helen Gahagan Douglas as "soft on Communism," a statement so dubious it earned him lifelong enemies.

Nixon and his running mate, Maryland Governor Spiro T. Agnew, took office under a "suspended judgment" of the American people. The

country was looking for a swift and equitable settlement to the conflict in Southeast Asia, an end to the student unrest that the continuation of the war had touched off on nearly every college campus in the country, and a quelling of the growing black militant movement that had sprung from the racial tensions of the 1960s.

While Nixon did not dismantle the New Frontier and Great Society programs of the two previous administrations, he did not build on them, either. His domestic policies tended to founder because of his failure to consider the enormous effect the civil rights movement of the 1960s had had on the country and public policy. The war in Vietnam continued to escalate as well—based on the President's and Secretary of Defense Henry Kissinger's decision to bomb Cambodia, in hopes that such a move would prevent enemy troops and supplies from entering South Vietnam by that route.

The President who pledged to bring the American people together, to end their divisiveness over the war and the racial hostilities that had racked the Johnson administration, then stunned the public by nominating to the Supreme Court G. Harrold Carswell, whom the Senate found unacceptable due to critical flaws in his handling of judicial cases that involved racial matters. Five months before, Nixon's nomination of Clement Haynsworth had been rejected for what one Senator described as a "mediocre" judicial record.

In fact, the courts turned out to be a major source of contention for President Nixon throughout his terms in office. Not only was Nixon the only President in the twentieth century to have two consecutive Supreme Court nominees rejected by the Senate, but because of the Supreme Court, the President failed to find a way to restrain the press, the group he viewed as most antagonistic to his administration. A significant incident, which resulted in forging a whole new area of freedom of the press, has come to be called the Pentagon Papers case.

In the spring of 1971, Daniel Ellsberg, a former Defense Department employee, leaked classified documents from a Pentagon study of the U.S. involvement in Vietnam. Although the study was not prepared by the Nixon administration, the State Department viewed its secrecy as vital to current negotiations to end the war. When the *New York Times* and the *Washington Post* began publishing articles and documents from the study in mid-June of that year, the government quickly enjoined the newspapers from exposing the information in the interest of "national security." In a swift display of justice, seventeen days later the Supreme Court upheld the *Times* and *Post* positions against the government's attempt at prior restraint.

Yet while domestic policy was not Nixon's strong suit, he proved to be a master at foreign policy issues. The ability and self-confidence he did not demonstrate in domestic matters blossomed in his handling of international affairs. His first summer in office he visited Rumania, making a major diplomatic breakthrough as the first American President to set foot in a communist country since President Truman conferred with Allied leaders at Potsdam (now in East Germany) in the closing days of World War II. The following summer, Egypt and Israel were induced to accept a cease-fire agreement to their conflict along the Suez Canal. But the dramatic triumph of President Nixon's foreign policy was his recognizing the government of the People's Republic of China with his state visit to Peking in February 1972. Many historians have said that Richard Nixon, the old "Cold Warrior" and staunch anti-communist of the 1950s, who was respected by foreign leaders for his knowledge of international affairs, was the only President who could have opened diplomatic relations with that major communist power. More importantly, Nixon knew this normalization of relations with what was then the government of Mao Tse-tung would provide the impetus for the easing of tensions between the U.S. and the Soviet Union.

Having no legislative record of the first term with which to impress voters, and an equally poor fiscal record in light of an economic recession that forced the President to enact emergency wage and price constraints during the summer of 1971, Nixon's ability for foreign policy carried him through the 1972 election against the Democratic challenger George McGovern, a liberal, anti-war senator from South Dakota. The incumbent's landslide victory over McGovern was so devastating it nearly wrecked the liberal wing of the Democratic Party. The President was re-elected carrying the electoral votes of every state in the nation except Massachusetts, home of the influential liberal Democratic Senator Edward (Ted) Kennedy, brother of both the assassinated President and New York Senator Robert F. Kennedy, assassinated while campaigning for the 1968 Democratic presidential nomination.

The satisfaction of the victory did not last long, however, before the press and the courts, the alternating thorns of this administration, brought down the man who yearned for greatness. For months before the election there had been rumblings from the press connecting high level officials of the Nixon administration and the re-election campaign to a seemingly insignificant burglary into the Democratic National Party Headquarters in the Watergate office complex in Washington in which five men were arrested on June 17, 1972. Eventually several top White House staff members, advisors, and Cabinet officers were indicted and convicted as conspirators in covering up the illegal activity which was, in fact, planned and paid for by the Committee to Re-elect the President, headed by former Attorney General John Mitchell. A special prosecutor was appointed to investigate the conflicting stories that abounded. In a tug of war for information with the Senate that lasted several months, President Nixon refused to turn over tape recorded conversations with his aides that could have provided the information the Senate wanted. It became clear that not only were they involved, but that Nixon knew about the break-in at the Watergate four days after it had taken place and had directed an effort to cover the trail.

As the investigation heated up a year after re-election, Vice President Agnew was indicted and later convicted of accepting payoffs for contracts offered by the State of Maryland while he was governor. He resigned on October 10, 1973, and Congressman Gerald Ford of Michigan, House Minority Leader, was appointed Vice President. Later that month, as disclosures continued before a Senate committee on the Watergate break-in and cover-up, twenty-two bills were introduced in Congress calling for an investigation of whether the President should be impeached. In late July 1974 the House Judiciary Committee approved three articles of impeachment charging Nixon with attempting to cover-up the Watergate burglary. A week later he released transcripts of recordings sought by the investigating committees. The evidence was damaging. It proved that the President had lied all along about his own and his staff's involvement in the burglary and the illegal payments made to finance the action and cover-up. Impeachment in the House and conviction by the Senate were virtual certainties.

On August 9, 1974 Richard Nixon resigned and left the White House with the dream of accomplishments to come in his second term shattered.

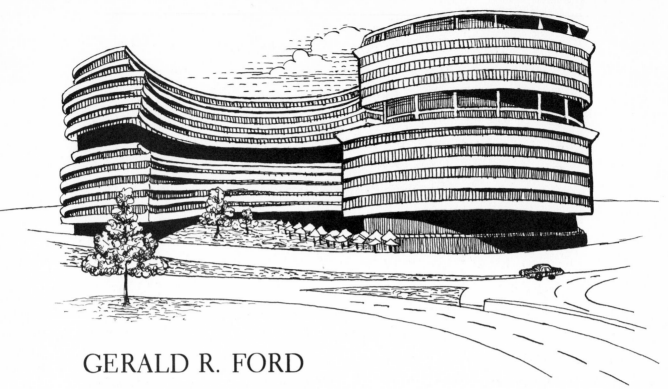

GERALD R. FORD

"Healing a Wounded Nation"

ON AUGUST 9, 1974, the day Richard Nixon resigned in the face of certain impeachment for his connection with the Watergate scandal, Gerald Ford became President. His ascension to the office began eight months earlier under the most unusual circumstances of any before him.

A Congressman for twenty-five years, and House Minority Leader, Ford was appointed Vice President by President Nixon when Spiro Agnew resigned following charges that he accepted payoffs while he was governor of Maryland. From that position, Ford then replaced a President also accused of crimes for which he left office under threat of prosecution.

So Gerald Ford saw his role as a President who would need to restore faith in government to the American people, who had their trust shaken by two national leaders. With the modesty that characterized his

234

demeanor, Gerald Ford told the nation he would do his best to lead it out of a sad period, just as Abraham Lincoln led the country out of the sad time of the Civil War. But, he said that he could not be equated with that great leader in more than his resolve. Then, drawing on a metaphor appropriate for someone from a state whose major industry is automobiles, added that he was, "a Ford, not a Lincoln."

When he took office the special prosecution team was still investigating Richard Nixon's role in the Watergate scandal. Several of the former President's aides were on trial for their part in it. A month later, with reporters at press conferences obsessed with his plans for Nixon, and headlines of the continuing investigation monopolizing the news, President Ford realized that he would be unable to get on with the pressing problems of his administration unless he forced the country to put the Watergate business behind it. To accomplish this goal, Gerald Ford pardoned former President Nixon for his offenses in connection with Watergate. President Ford has written that his motivation for pardoning Nixon did not stem from compassion but from concern that the national addiction to this controversy had created a destructive and divisive debate of lasting bitterness. Yet he did not expect the cry of public opinion that went up after the pardon. He thought the American people would realize that this controversy had carried on too long. He expected them to have more compassion for the Nixon family. Instead he heard people all over the country protest the pardon, many comparing it to nearly meaningless limited amnesty he tried to give to young men who fled the country to avoid the draft during the Vietnam War.

Although the American people were looking for a new leader and wanted Gerald Ford to succeed, his administration—certainly from the time he granted the pardon—was beset with severe difficulties. Stepping into the Presidency so abruptly, the man who had been a stand-in Vice President did not have adequate transition time to form his priorities and attack them systematically. Then, although he was well known and well respected by Congress as a member of that body for many years, he was a relatively conservative Republican working with a liberal Democratic Congress that wanted to limit the President's powers in reaction to what they saw as Nixon's excesses. He also was extremely conscious of not having the mandate of a successful election to support his decisions on bleak economic and political situations. The economy was inflation-ridden and greatly affected by the oil embargo from the Middle East in the fall of 1973. Tensions with the Soviet Union increased as the previously negotiated detente eroded. The Paris peace talks concerning the U.S. retreat from Vietnam were making little progress. In addition, the U.S. became involved in mediating a possible war between Greece and Turkey over the Turks' invasion of the island of Cyprus.

The economic situation continued to deteriorate as the price of petroleum products rose every few months during this period and the public soon came to view Gerald Ford as ineffective against these staggering problems. Although he had promised his wife, Betty, that he would retire from public life in January 1977, he decided to run for President in 1976. He chose as his running mate former New York Governor Nelson Rockefeller, whom he had appointed Vice President to fill his own vacancy. But Ford never recovered the popularity loss he suffered following the pardon of Richard Nixon and he narrowly lost the election.

The 895 days of the Ford administration were not a full term, but they were filled with enough drama for two terms. When the merchant ship the U.S.S. Mayaguez was seized by the Cambodians in international waters off that Southeast Asian country, President Ford's decision to begin air strikes and call in the Marines to rescue the crew resulted in heavy casualties. He oversaw the humiliating withdrawal of the American military from Vietnam. Mrs. Ford underwent an operation for cancer while they occupied the White House and the President was seriously concerned for her health. Then, on two occasions, he was the

subject of assassination attempts. It all might have been too harrowing for a football hero from a small town in the Midwest.

Gerald Rudolph Ford, Jr., was born Leslie L. King, Jr., on July 14, 1913 in Omaha, Neb. His parents divorced when he was three years old and shortly thereafter his mother married Gerald Rudolph Ford of Grand Rapids, Michigan, who adopted the boy and changed his name. The Fords subsequently had three more sons whom they instilled with three basic rules: be honest, work hard, and come to dinner on time. Young Gerald Ford worked his way through the University of Michigan where he majored in economics and political science and played football for the famous Wolverines. Upon graduation he took a position as assistant football coach and freshman boxing coach at Yale University. Two years later he convinced the deans to allow him to attend Yale Law School while still keeping the coaching job to pay his expenses.

After law school, he opened a small practice in Grand Rapids, and became active in local politics. Following a stint in the Navy in World War II, he was elected to Congress in 1948. There he remained the tireless and dedicated Representative from Michigan until he was appointed Vice President. Even when he was President, Gerald Ford referred to the House of Representatives as "home." Collective, democratic, government had become his style, and he found the solitary decision-making of the presidency often disturbing.

Upon leaving the White House in January 1977, the former President, healthy and at the height of his career, received several attractive job offers. The one that appealed to him the most was from the American Enterprise Institute for Public Policy Research, a "think tank" in Washington, D.C. As a member of the institute, Ford has traveled to twenty university campuses a year to talk to students and faculty about foreign affairs, national defense, American politics, and the economy.

JAMES EARL CARTER
"The Human Rights Advocate"

JAMES Earl, ("Jimmy") Carter was born on October 1, 1924 in Plains, Georgia to James Earl Sr. and Lillian Carter, who owned a peanut warehousing business. James Sr. had a varied career in which he managed a grocery, owned an ice house and dry cleaner, bought land, sold farm supplies, and even held office as a representative to the Georgia State Legislature. Young James attended Georgia Southwestern University, Georgia Institute of Technology, and received his undergraduate degree at the U.S. Naval Academy in 1947; subsequently he did graduate work at Union College. In the Navy he advanced from ensign to lieutenant and retired in 1953 to return to the family business. Active in local politics, Jimmy Carter served in the Georgia State Senate from 1962 to 1966. He ran for governor and lost in 1966 before attaining the office in the 1970 election. After one term he again returned to peanut farming and warehousing but remained active in Democratic party politics. A devout Baptist, the state senator, governor, and presidential candidate was a deacon and Sunday school teacher at the Plains Baptist Church until his election to the Presidency.

240

Carter was elected on a wave of public sentiment that sought to sweep the Republicans from Washington. The Carter administration attempted to "clean up" politics in this country—while also trying to correct the chronic inflation and unemployment that plagued the nation's economy.

Reluctantly, Carter and his new administration guaranteed federal loans to the Chrysler corporation, which was suffering from slumping automobile sales in the face of constantly rising gasoline prices. The administration feared that for a corporation of Chrysler's size and reputation to go bankrupt would drastically affect an already troubled economy. All of the major auto manufacturers in the country were ailing. The gas crisis caused a loss of sales to more fuel-efficient Japanese models; and all were threatening to lay off workers by the thousands.

Despite his valiant efforts, however, Carter was not able to hold the line on inflation and unemployment, and in the second half of his term in office, the nation slipped deeper into a recession. Yet, an anti-*status quo* feeling prevailed in Washington, and fueled Carter's bold attempts to rid government of corruption and excess bureaucracy.

His critics maintain that Carter missed an opportunity to strike a blow for the country's energy independence, a looming factor in the high cost of living, runaway inflation, and distressing unemployment and interest rates. Although he created a new Cabinet position to deal with energy issues, The Department of Energy was fraught with problems, and the president had no firm energy policy, which many business and industry leaders felt would be a major step on the road to economic recovery.

Although many people saw Carter's foreign policy as one that weakened the image of the United States in the eyes of other countries, time seems to be proving that he had the correct perspective on international relations. Carter saw that the world had changed vastly since World War II, when this country managed its affairs by wielding its military might against those who disagreed with the American way. He felt the United States had become interdependent with, not independent of, the rest of the world, and that the show of military strength was a futile gesture and one unbecoming to a world power. He realized that if there was to be world peace, we had to learn to negotiate with other nations from a position of equality, not as a superpower making demands on a dependent nation. This attitude became clear in his battle for human rights around the globe. The President felt strongly that those countries who deny their citizens basic human rights—including freedom to criticize their leaders and freedom from political repression—would not receive economic or political assistance from Americans. He was particularly critical of Central and South American countries, such as Argentina, Chile, El Salvador, and others which were run by dictatorships or military juntas.

The test of this human rights policy came when the Soviet government invaded Afghanistan on its southern border in 1980. Soviet leaders justified the invasion and occupation on the grounds that Afghanistan's government was unstable and hostile to the Soviet Union's security. President Carter quickly moved to cut off our grain shipments to the Soviet Union. The Soviets needed the grain because farmers there do not grow enough for a year-round supply, for much of the country which has an unusually long winter season.

In the course of the Carter administration's turbulent years, many critics commented on its performance. But more thoughtful voices have wondered since whether anyone could have handled the monumental problems that his administration faced. The worst of the catastrophes to befall the country while he was in office was certainly the capture of fifty-two Americans by the revolutionary government of Iran just before Thanksgiving of 1979. A fundamentalist Moslem group was angry because President Carter admitted the Shah of Iran to the U.S. for medical treatment before he died.

The group, led by the Islamic clergyman Ayatollah Ruhollah Khomeini—drove the Shah, Reza Pahlavi, and his family from Iran for using oppressive political and military tactics against critics of his regime. As a government friendly to the Shah, the United States tried to find him a home in exile. Angered by the assistance the Americans were giving their deposed leader, the Iranians seized the American embassy in November and held fifty men and two women hostage for fourteen months in the compound of buildings in Teheran, the country's capital.

It has become clear in the aftermath of this incident that American leaders who attempted to negotiate the hostages' release missed several important signals, and may have prolonged the crisis. Eventually, however, with the help of several members of the international diplomatic community all of the hostages were released—but not until well after the 1980 election. The hostage crisis weighed as heavily on the minds of the voters as they went to the polls in November as it did on President Carter's shoulders. And with the President's confidence undermined by this terrible reality, as well as the worsening economic situation, he and Vice President Walter Mondale lost the election to the conservative Republican challenger, former California governor Ronald Reagan and his running mate George Bush.

One of President Carter's few satisfactions in those final days in office was that he was able to extricate the hostages in a very sensitive bargain with the government of Iran before his term officially ended. And graciously, incoming President Reagan sent Jimmy Carter to greet the hostages in West Germany after their release.

RONALD W. REAGAN

"Western Individualism"

TAKING office as the fortieth President sixteen days before his seventieth birthday, Ronald Reagan is the oldest man elected to the American Presidency. He also stands out among his predecessors in that he is also the first former movie actor to be elected to the post. But like many who filled the office before him, he is a former state governor.

After retiring from acting in the early 1960s, Ronald Reagan made a successful career change to politics and was elected to the state house of California in 1967. He viewed his six years there as the best training ground for the Presidency, as he believes California to be a microcosm of the rest of the country—a state that has both agriculture and business interests, national parks and wilderness areas alongside vast urban centers, and a generally heterogeneous population.

Not only was the election of Ronald Reagan and his Vice President, George Bush, an indication of the country's dissatisfaction with

246

the policies of the Democratic party and the Carter administration, but it may also indicate a public sentiment that runs in favor of a more traditional system of values—the tried and true.

Thus far, Mr. Reagan's chief priority has been to reduce federal spending, drastically altering the role of government in the regulation of business, social welfare programs, and federal services, believing such a program to be the quickest road to economic recovery and the slowing of inflation. In addition, he has also sought to strengthen the American image abroad, taking a staunch anti-communist stance in foreign affairs, and concentrating more money and effort in military and defense areas.

An individualist in the tradition of the pioneers who travelled west across the country more than a century before, Ronald Reagan headed west to California from Tampico, Illinois, to seek his fortune following graduation from Eureka College, where he majored in economics and enjoyed a short career as a local sports announcer.

He made his way as a struggling film actor in Hollywood and eventually appeared as a leading man or principal player in a number of movies in the 1940s and 1950s. After his first marriage to actress Jane Wyman ended in divorce, he was elected as president to the Screen Actors Guild, a union for film performers. As president of that organization, he cooperated with Senator Joe McCarthy of Minnesota in his attempts to keep communists from working in the film industry.

During this period he met and married Nancy Davis, a young actress and the daughter of a well to do family. He developed many new contacts, and met with many influential people who shared his political philosophy, and who eventually supported him in his bid for the governorship of California.

After his term as governor, he then made an unsuccessful try for the Republican Presidential nomination in 1976, losing to incumbent President Gerald Ford. His patience and accurate assessment of public sentiment were rewarded, however, in 1980. He pledged to lead the country down the road to economic recovery and to lessen the taxpayer's burden by reducing big government.

President Reagan faces the dilemma of a volatile world situation that includes a possibility of continued trouble in the Middle East, and protests from our Western European allies against the placing of United States defense systems—particularily missiles—in their countries. Domestic budget deficits threaten to increase in the next years, and perhaps what can be called a less-than-confident attitude on the part of American business interests currently exists towards his economic policies. It remains to be seen how the western pioneer spirit of Ronald Reagan will fare in the light of a troubled modern world.

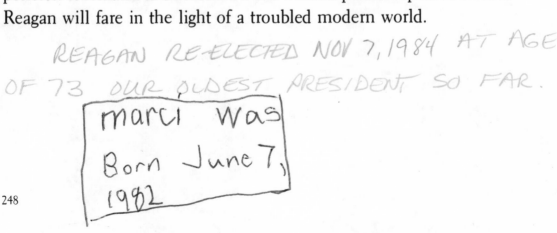

REAGAN RE-ELECTED NOV 7, 1984 AT AGE
OF 73 OUR OLDEST PRESIDENT SO FAR.

marci was
Born June 7,
1982

248

PRESIDENT	TERM OF OFFICE
1. George Washington	Apr. 30, 1789—Mar. 3, 1797
2. John Adams	Mar. 4, 1797—Mar. 3, 1801
3. Thomas Jefferson	Mar. 4, 1801—Mar. 3, 1805
	Mar. 4, 1805—Mar. 3, 1809
4. James Madison	Mar. 4, 1809—Mar. 3, 1813
	Mar. 4, 1813—Mar. 3, 1817
5. James Monroe	Mar. 4, 1817—Mar. 3, 1825
6. John Quincy Adams	Mar. 4, 1825—Mar. 3, 1829
7. Andrew Jackson	Mar. 4, 1829—Mar. 3, 1833
	Mar. 4, 1833—Mar. 3, 1837
8. Martin Van Buren	Mar. 4, 1837—Mar. 3, 1841
9. William Henry Harrison	Mar. 4, 1841—Apr. 4, 1841
10. John Tyler	Apr. 6, 1841—Mar. 3, 1845
11. James Knox Polk	Mar. 4, 1845—Mar. 3, 1849
12. Zachary Taylor	Mar. 5, 1849—July 9, 1850
13. Millard Fillmore	July 10, 1850—Mar. 3, 1853
14. Franklin Pierce	Mar. 4, 1853—Mar. 3, 1857
15. James Buchanan	Mar. 4, 1857—Mar. 3, 1861
16. Abraham Lincoln	Mar. 4, 1861—Mar. 3, 1865
	Mar. 4, 1865—Apr. 15, 1865
17. Andrew Johnson	Apr. 15, 1865—Mar. 3, 1869
18. Ulysses S. Grant	Mar. 4, 1869—Mar. 3, 1873
	Mar. 4, 1873—Mar. 3, 1877
19. Rutherford B. Hayes	Mar. 4, 1877—Mar. 3, 1881
20. James A. Garfield	Mar. 4, 1881—Sept. 19, 1881

21.	Chester A. Arthur	Sept. 20, 1881—Mar. 3, 1885
22.	Grover Cleveland	Mar. 4, 1885—Mar. 3, 1889
23.	Benjamin Harrison	Mar. 4, 1889—Mar. 3, 1893
24.	Grover Cleveland	Mar. 4, 1893—Mar. 3, 1897
25.	William McKinley	Mar. 4, 1897—Mar. 3, 1901
		Mar. 4, 1901—Sept. 14, 1901
26.	Theodore Roosevelt	Sept. 14, 1901—Mar. 3, 1905
		Mar. 4, 1905—Mar. 3, 1909
27.	William Howard Taft	Mar. 4, 1909—Mar. 3, 1913
28.	Woodrow Wilson	Mar. 4, 1913—Mar. 3, 1921
29.	Warren G. Harding	Mar. 4, 1921—Aug. 2, 1923
30.	Calvin Coolidge	Aug. 3, 1923—Mar. 3, 1925
		Mar. 4, 1925—Mar. 3, 1929
31.	Herbert C. Hoover	Mar. 4, 1929—Mar. 3, 1933
32.	Franklin D. Roosevelt	Mar. 4, 1933—Jan. 20, 1941
		Jan. 20, 1941—Jan. 20, 1945
		Jan. 20, 1945—Apr. 12, 1945
33.	Harry S. Truman	Apr. 12, 1945—Jan. 20, 1949
		Jan. 20, 1949—Jan. 20, 1953
34.	Dwight D. Eisenhower	Jan. 20, 1953—Jan. 20, 1957
		Jan. 20, 1957—Jan. 20, 1961
35.	John F. Kennedy	Jan. 20, 1961—Nov. 22, 1963
36.	Lyndon B. Johnson	Nov. 22, 1963—Jan. 20, 1965
		Jan. 20, 1965—Jan. 20, 1969
37.	Richard M. Nixon	Jan. 20, 1969—Jan. 20, 1973
		Jan. 20, 1973—Aug. 9, 1974
38.	Gerald R. Ford	Aug. 9, 1974—Jan. 20, 1977
39.	Jimmy (James Earl) Carter	Jan. 20, 1977—Jan. 20, 1981
40.	Ronald Reagan	Jan. 20, 1981—

INTERESTING FACTS ABOUT THE PRESIDENTS

- John Adams and John Quincy Adams were the only father and son to both hold the office of President.

- Two Presidents were grandfather and grandson: William Henry Harrison and Benjamin Harrison.

- Grover Cleveland is the only President to have a child born in the White House.

- John Tyler had the most children of any President—fifteen.

- Jimmy Carter was the first President to have been born in a hospital. All of the previous Presidents had been born at home.

- William H. Taft was the largest President. He stood over six feet tall, and weighed 350 pounds.

- James Madison was the smallest President, standing just under five feet, four inches tall, and weighing only about one hundred pounds.

- George Washington and James Madison were the only two Presidents who also signed the Constitution.

- John Adams was the first President to live in the White House.

- James Buchanan was the only President who never married.

- President Andrew Johnson never went to school; he was a runaway indentured servant, and did not learn reading and writing until his wife taught him.

- Theodore Roosevelt was the first President to visit a foreign country while in office.

- Martin Van Buren was the first President to be born in the United States. Prior to that, all seven previous Presidents had been born in the "English Colonies."

- Woodrow Wilson was the only President to hold a doctoral degree—a Ph.D.

- The first President to speak on radio was Woodrow Wilson. The first to appear on television was Franklin Roosevelt.

- Lyndon Johnson was the only President to be sworn into office on an airplane.

- Grover Cleveland is the only President to serve two nonconsecutive terms in office.

- Gerald Ford is the only President never to have won an election for either President or Vice President.

- Abraham Lincoln was defeated in bids for public office six times before becoming President.

- Andrew Jackson was the first President to be nominated by a national political convention.

- Only once have a President and his Vice President been members of different political parties. It happened in 1797, when Thomas Jefferson, a Republican, became Vice President under John Adams, a Federalist.

- Richard Nixon is the only man to have resigned the office of President.

- Nixon is also the only man to serve as President who also served as Vice President, but who did not succeed the President under whom he served.

- William Howard Taft served as both President and as Chief Justice of the Supreme Court.

- Taft is also the only President who administered the Oath of Office to two of his successors, Calvin Coolidge and Herbert Hoover.

- Three Presidents have lost the popular vote, yet won the electoral vote: John Quincy Adams, 1824; Rutherford B. Hayes, 1876; and Benjamin Harrison, 1888.

- Franklin Delano Roosevelt was the man to hold the office for the longest period of time: twelve years, one month and eight days.

- William Henry Harrison served only one month in office.

- John Adams and Herbert Hoover are the only two Presidents to live past the age of ninety.

- John Kennedy was the President who died the youngest; at age forty-six.

- Three Presidents have died on the Fourth of July; Thomas Jefferson, John Adams and James Monroe.

- John Adams and Thomas Jefferson died on the same day—July 4, 1826.

Between 1840 and 1960, every President elected at twenty-year intervals has died in office. Who were they? William Henry Harrison, Abraham Lincoln, James A. Garfield, William McKinley, Franklin Delano Roosevelt, and John F. Kennedy.

Four Presidents have been assassinated while in office: Abraham Lincoln, James Garfield, William McKinley, and John Kennedy.

THE OATH OF OFFICE

I do solemnly swear that I will faithfully execute the Office of the President of the United States, and will, to the best of my ability, preserve, protect, and defend the Constitution of the United States.